DISCOVER
DUBLIN

DISCOVER DUBLIN

HUGH LAMBERT

The Collins Press

Published in 2016 by
The Collins Press
West Link Park
Doughcloyne
Wilton
Cork
T12 N5EF
Ireland

First published by Magpie 2015

A CIP record for this book is available from the British Library

Paperback ISBN: 978-1-84889-296-5

Design and typesetting by John Lambert
Typeset in Caslon

Cover design by John Lambert

Printed in Poland by Białostockie Zakłady Graficzne SA

Prrevious pages: Bookshelves at Trinity College Library, Dublin, Ireland.

CONTENTS

Foreword   7

1. Iveagh Gardens   10
    True Dubs: Buck Whaley   14

2. Poolbeg Lighthouse   16
    True Dubs: Grizell Steevens   22

3. The Martello Towers   24
    True Dubs: Arthur Wellesley   30

4. Smithfield Fruit and Vegetable Market   32
    True Dubs: Arthur Guinness   38

5. Dún Laoghaire   40
    True Dubs: Charles Robert Maturin   48

6. Christ Church   50
    True Dubs: James Clarence Mangan   56

7. Phoenix Park   58
    True Dubs: Henry Grattan   64

8. Trinity College   66
    True Dubs: Bram Stoker   72

9. Killiney Hill   74
    True Dubs: Patrick Sarsfield   80

10. Clontarf   82
    True Dubs: Cathal Brugha   90

11. The Dublin Mountains   92
    True Dubs: Sinéad de Valera   98

12. Temple Bar   102
    True Dubs: Lucien Bull   110

13. Donabate 112

    True Dubs: Molesworth Phillips 118

14. Museums 120

    True Dubs: Catherine McAuley 128

15. Dublin Castle 130

    True Dubs: Frederick Maning 138

16. Lambay Island 140

    True Dubs: Seán Lemass 146

17. O'Connell Street 148

    True Dubs: Christian Davies 154

18. Sandymount 156

    True Dubs: John Dowland 162

19. Botanic Gardens 164

    True Dubs: Brian O'Nolan 170

20. Howth 172

    True Dubs: Dermot McMurrough 178

21. Chapelizod, Lucan & Leixlip 180

    True Dubs: Sheridan Le Fanu 186

22. St Stephen's Green 188

    True Dubs: Tom Kettle 196

FOREWORD

If while out walking in this city the reader were to seize a passing historian and ask: what intrigues you the most? They may be surprised to find the answer is not Ancient Egypt, the Coliseum or far-flung Machu Picchu, but what lies all around them. From the foot-worn pavements to the castellated rooftops the city of Dublin heaves with age and curios enough to fire the most jaded of urban imaginations.

The thoughts of the ordinary person as he or she looks about their world have been voiced through the medium of journalism in the shape of social and political commentaries for some time now. But, as any history lover knows, to understand truly who we are we must learn first about where we came from and how we got here. In short, the past is all around us and it's definitely worth having a look.

It was in that journalistic form that the chapters in this book were first digested as articles by the Irish public in the mid 1990s, through *The Leader* newspaper and one long-serving journalist and writer, Hugh Lambert.

A short-lived publication, *The Leader* struggled to find what light it could to thrive in the early years of the economic boom and Hugh, being the enthusiastic and imaginative journalist he was, chose to indulge his passion for history and his native city by treating the readership to weekly excursions around the curious corners and forgotten alcoves, to the unusual histories and infamous characters of the great city of Dublin.

Twenty-two articles were produced about historic Dublin and its environs and, coupled with amusing profiles of some outrageous past denizens it proved to be hugely popular with the urban community at the time. The expanding and increasingly cosmopolitan populace of Dublin in the mid 1990s was happy to hear of another park besides St Stephen's Green to lounge about in of a summer's day, or a hidden history secreted about their daily commute in the bustling capital port.

However, it was Hugh's own writing style that engaged so many readers during the column's brief existence, and it is in no small part the reason that we, his family, have decided to gather the articles together into this book. Some details have been updated but each article is essentially as it was originally published. There's a personable ease and breeziness with which Hugh enjoys his subject and a feeling that he is rather pleased you've decided to let him show you around.

So to the family, friends and colleagues who knew him this will hopefully be a welcome, and long overdue, tribute to a wonderful writer, enthusiastic antiquarian and all-round likeable fellow as he invites you on a stroll through his favourite city: his very own, and very interesting, city of Dublin.

Paul Lambert
P.S. And for those of you new to Hugh, turn the page and say how do you do!

Sackville Street (now O'Connell Street), taken from *Magasin Pittoresque*, Paris, 1882

The Secret Garden
in Our City Centre

Iveagh Gardens

SO, you know Dublin. Answer these questions, then: is there a public park no more than two minutes' walk from St Stephen's Green? Is it half the size of the Green? Does it have two large fountains, a waterfall, a maze and an archery arena?

Yes, yes and – yes, yes, yes and yes. The Iveagh Gardens is one of the city's best kept secrets. They've been sitting there in secluded peace for over two centuries since they were first laid out for John Scott, otherwise the Earl of Clonmell. An MP and lawyer, Clonmell was popularly known as 'copper-faced Jack' because of his cheek and his permanently tanned complexion. He rose to dizzy heights in Anglo-Irish society, finally landing the position of Chief Justice and, along the way, acquiring the reputation of being a hanging judge.

In the nineteenth century, the gardens passed into the hands of the Guinness family and it was in 1939 that Rupert Edward

Cecil Lee of that clan, otherwise the second Lord Iveagh, gave his Palladian house on the Green to the Government and the Gardens to University College Dublin (UCD). The house became the Department of External Affairs – later Foreign Affairs. The Gardens slumbered on as a pleasure reserved for a favoured few. These 11 sleepy acres – the Green is about 22 acres – are tucked away in the middle of the rectangle formed by the south side of the Green, Harcourt Street, Ely Place and Hatch Street. Go up Harcourt Street from the Green. Just past the Children's Hospital you will find a short cul-de-sac – Clonmel Street, named after his aforementioned nibs – and at the end of it an elderly stone wall with stately black gates. If they're open, you're in.

Until a couple of years ago, the Iveagh Gardens were known only to UCD inmates of the pre-Belfield era. The College allowed its staff and students to use the leafy oasis as a fair-weather retreat. Much book work was done in its open patches, under the elms, oaks and chestnuts by those who would become the country's scholars, physicians, architects and lawyers. No doubt much else took place as well. During these years the Gardens, already fairly run down when UCD took them over, fell further into neglect. Ivy, appropriately enough, spread everywhere.

When UCD handed the park over to the Office of Public Works (OPW) a few years ago, the paperwork mentioned that the

Gardens contained a waterfall, two large fountains and a child's maze. Where were they, wondered the OPW. Had they ever existed? What could have happened to them?

After a general dusting down, a clearing of decades of autumn leaves and a pruning-back of the rampant ivy, the Gardens' overgrown impedimenta began to reappear. There, on either side of the main avenue, two 10-foot statues stood in the centre of two circular ponds, each bearing aloft a large bowl which once overflowed with water.

Off to the right the remains of the maze revealed itself. And round the corner from the entrance, behind a great bank of foliage was found the dried-up waterfall – a rocky grotto with two broken Roman deities.

Now the water flows again from the two fountains and new pipes are being laid to allow the waterfall to sparkle again. And the maze is forming again with newly planted miniature hedging.

When all's ready, the OPW will introduce Dubliners once again to this forgotten delight. In the meantime, the Gardens are open to the public. If you love the city, you'll love the Iveagh Gardens. But don't all go on the same day.

Buck Whaley

TRUE DUBS

BEING a bon viveur and general rascal, he was an unusual pilgrim to the Holy Land. The journey was an extravagant and perilous undertaking in the late eighteenth century but Thomas Whaley never liked to turn down an interesting wager.

If he could do the journey from Dublin to Jerusalem and back home within a year, he would be richer by £20,000. He made it in nine months, arriving back to glory in June 1789.

Variously known as Buck Whaley and Jerusalem Whaley, he was born in 1766 with a silver spoon in his mouth in one of the fine houses on St Stephen's Green. At thirteen, he found himself bestowed with £60,000 in cash and an income of £7,000 a year.

So it was off to Paris for a gentleman's education. His tutor managed to impart a modicum of knowledge, but failed utterly to divert his young charge from his gambling habits. Whaley ran through vast sums of money and soon had to head for home. The Jerusalem caper helped him to set himself up again in accustomed style. He was but twenty-three.

Flamboyant, opinionated and unscrupulous, Whaley landed himself a seat in parliament. He voted for the Union and later voted against it – the word was that the young scoundrel was easily bribed.

Buck Whaley lived a short and spectacular life. He died in 1800 at just thirty-four years of age in Cheshire while on his way to London. Years later it emerged that, in private memoirs which were finally published in 1905, he felt much remorse at his unprincipled life.

2

Walk on the Wild Side!

Poolbeg Lighthouse

MOST Dubliners have seen it from a distance, but how many have walked the South Wall to the Poolbeg Lighthouse? The Liffey, like wine, women and song, can be enjoyed in many different ways. From the featherbeddy springs up by Kippure, through the opulent fields of Kildare, to the stony curves of the city quays, it is perhaps the fundamental treasure of Dublin.

It's in the nature of decent rivers that they are at their most impressive, most majestic where they expire into the open sea. And the Liffey is certainly splendid down in its breathy wide-open death throes between Clontarf and Ringsend.

Once it was called the *Ruirtheach*, the sparkling flood or cascade. Then it became *Abhainn Life*. The story goes that on their way to Tara from the south wealthy Deltbanna Mac Drucht and wife Liffe came upon a river of great beauty. Liffe, who was of course another great beauty, asked her husband to name it after her. He did and the men

> Ever since ships had sailed into Dublin, the Bay was infamous as a dangerous and deadly place.

of Erin complied rather than suffer the deprivation of drink which Deltbanna threatened.

The Liffey may not be a great river in length, but it is certainly great in lore. One of the best places to drink in its spirit, metaphorically, is the place where it ends its purpose, where it fans out to feed the sea. And there, in the South Wall, we have the perfect promenade to bring us right out into the heart of this endless lively death. This great man-made finger of stone has its seasons. It has its balmy days, occasionally, but it's more usually a splendidly invigorating excursion, one which is surprisingly little known among dedicated Dubliners.

Whether you approach it from the north or south city, you must pass through the bleak and deserted roads of the south port which once teemed with small coal merchants and family boatyards. Persist through this Stygian wasteland and, as you near the Pigeon House, the high-sky magic of the place begins to make itself felt.

Ever since ships first sailed into Dublin, the bay was infamous as a dangerous and deadly place. Two great sand banks – the North Bull and the South Bull – were forever changing shape and further out there were the reefs of Howth and Dalkey. All sorts of suggestions were made. One proposed that old Dunleary be made the out-port for Dublin, with a canal connecting it to the city. This idea was briefly entertained, but it was probably Captain William Bligh, later to be the ill-fated master of HMS *Bounty*, who delivered the *coup de grâce*.

'Breadfruit' Bligh, so called because he had accompanied Captain Cook on his South Seas voyage which brought the breadfruit to Europe, was a noted navigator and surveyor. He felt that the canal idea effectively meant the abandonment of Dublin as a port. Bligh was commissioned to perform an extensive survey of the bay and all its peculiarities. His superb work became the basis for the future development of Dublin Bay.

Before it had all been rendered safe, sailing ships were often forced by bad weather to let their passengers ashore 'at Mr Pidgeon's house'. Pidgeon – his first name seems to have escaped the records – was a port overseer who had been set up by the Ballast Board in a large home-cum-storehouse at the end of the first phase of the South Wall's extended construction programme. A man with an eye for business, he spotted the opportunities provided by the popularity of the South Wall project among Dubliners. Soon he and his family were laying on refreshments, boat outings and accommodation for the stream of city folk who wanted to see one of the world's great engineering projects taking shape before their eyes.

So, on past the Pigeon House and the ESB's huge red-and-white discharge chimneys. The road takes a few lefts and rights as it skirts the southern bay. After two small sandy beaches, one the famous Shelly Banks (although the shells have long vanished), you're on the wall proper, in its day one of the longest of its kind in the world. The last structures you'll pass are the ruins of the Battery, an old fort which once rang to cannon and anti-aircraft guns, and the square block of a defunct sewage terminal. Now you're marching out across the slabs of granite and limestone with the freshest air in Dublin filling your lungs.

To the left are the flat heaving waters of the Liffey dying in the grey-green sea. To the right the salty sea, never deep but always tossing waves against the works of man. Out to sea you go, out among the tugs of the river pilots, the big ferries and cargo vessels, out among the cormorants and the gulls. The Half Moon Swimming Club, now sadly bearing a freshly erected warning that these waters do not reach EU safety standards, marks half way. Nothing left now but the Wall and the huge red button of the Poolbeg Lighthouse at the end. If you're careful, and the sea and the wind are being reasonable, you can go down from the wall to the platform on which the lighthouse is built.

Here, of all places in Dublin, you feel the pleasing tension between man and nature, between the cocky pride of a beloved city

View of the Poolbeg towers across the Liffey from the North Wall and the power of tide and sand and wind which play along with the notion that they have been tamed. Stand at the end of the South Wall and turn the whole of Dublin before you. From the hook of Dalkey, across the soft Dublin Mountains, over the spires and towers of the city, on to Clontarf's line of square houses and broadleaf trees so thin between sea and sky, and finally to the great hump of Howth, lying forever in repose at the top of the bay. The South Wall: where Dubliners can get away from it all without leaving the city.

Grizell Steevens

TRUE DUBS

SHE could have squandered everything on the high life, but Grizell Steevens was made of finer stuff. Her twin brother, Richard, was one of the most successful physicians in Dublin during the closing years of the seventeenth century and when he died in 1710, he left his very large estate to her.

The fortune was Grizell's for life – but on her death it was to fund a hospital for the city's poor. Instead Grizell took just £100 a year for herself and set about realising her late brother's dream. Dr Steevens' Hospital was completed in 1733 on a site on the Liffey's south bank where Kingsbridge railway station (now Heuston Station) would rise over a century later. During the extended time it took to erect such a noble edifice, Grizell Steevens became the subject of talk around the city. It was said by cruel rumour-mongers that she had the face of a pig – she had once spurned a beggar who then imposed the porcine curse. None of this was true, of course, but those were credulous times.

Madam Steevens was not about to stand for this nonsense – she might not have been the greatest beauty Ireland had ever seen, but she was certainly no pig. She arranged for her own living quarters at the new hospital to be on the ground floor with a parlour window looking out on the street. There she would sit by the window, engaged in embroidery or other ladylike pursuits, with her face plainly visible to the world outside.

The hospital given to Dublin by the Steevens twins had grown very down-at-heel until the OPW went in boldly, refurbished the whole place, gave it a new front in full harmony with the original building. Well worth a visit.

The Granite Buttons on Dublin's Ragged Hem

The Martello Towers

WE have the name wrong. We should be calling them Mortella Towers. But it's an old mistake and time makes all things right. We'll always call the granite buttons on Dublin's ragged hem Martello Towers.

It was during the Napoleonic alarms that London decided we needed to be on our guard. The little Corsican was on a spectacular rampage in Europe, demolishing old nations and setting up new ones with cousins and nephews in nominal charge. No doubt he had his beady eye on Ireland.

The danger of a full-scale invasion by the French was very real – they had already tried it unsuccessfully at Bantry in 1796 and at Killala in 1798. Military men in London and Paris were fully alive to the strategic value of the softly defended and ever rebellious island just 60 nautical miles to the west of Britain.

> From Balbriggan to Bray they number a surprising twenty-one . . . on the southern sweep of Dublin Bay the Martellos are almost dense.

It was around 1802 that the decision was taken that the coasts needed something special by way of defence and early warning. A series of impregnable signal towers would be built, each within sight of the next. Dublin, being a particularly important place in the scheme of things, would get special attention. So, the gangs were assembled and the quarries were quarried. Men sweated and horses heaved through 1804 and 1805 with mighty tackle and monstrous chains, while across two seas Bonaparte made himself an emperor and Horatio Nelson wounded his pride at Trafalgar.

The Irish towers went up mostly along the coast of Dublin, but they were dotted here and there at other places in Cork, Donegal and the Shannon estuary. So well were they built that they stand as solidly as ever today despite much neglect. It's one of those pleasing ironies of history that we owe our Martello towers to the French in more ways than one.

The distinctive design – walls 40 feet high and 8 feet thick, single small entrances, flat roofs providing perfect firing platforms

– was suggested to England's war office by reports of a particularly difficult Mediterranean engagement some ten years earlier. Whom were the English fighting at the time? The French, of course. Where did this irrelevant battle take place? Yes, Corsica – at Cape Mortella! The old argument between the two nations had flared into new bitterness in 1793, the year the French beheaded Louis XVI.

At Mortella the English found themselves particularly hard pressed to drive the enemy out of a solid tower of granite. They hadn't seen this kind of fortification before and were not long about bringing news of it back to London – especially since the tale made them look all the braver. Ten years later Dublin was getting a job lot of these delightful but useless towers, mistakenly called Martello.

From Balbriggan to Bray they number a surprising twenty-one. Three are on islands – Shenick's Island off Skerries, Ireland's Eye and Dalkey Island. On the southern sweep of Dublin Bay the Martellos are almost dense – the Sandymount tower, now at last a restaurant, is followed by towers at Blackrock, Seapoint, Sandycove where James Joyce spent a night or two, and then Dalkey (not the island tower). South around the headland the towers resume with one overlooking Killiney beach and two more on either side of Bray.

Which leaves ten for the north side. First, the Red Rock tower, made of local red limestone rather than the usual granite. Then on around the peninsula for the splendidly sited tower above Howth

harbour. Portmarnock is next, followed by the lovely Malahide tower softened by ivy and a conical roof added long after the garrison had dispersed.

The Donabate peninsula has two towers, the first right marking the coast's change from sand to stone, the second right at the point of the arrowhead. On to Rush and then Loughshinny – this tower is on a headland which, some speculate, might have been a short-lived Roman foothold. And that leaves the towers at Skerries and Balbriggan. Enumerating the towers is a perilous undertaking. The fury of a woman scorned is nothing as compared to that of the Dublin pedant whose Martello has been overlooked.

No doubt you'll let us know if we've got it wrong.

Arthur Wellesley

TRUE DUBS

ALTHOUGH he was educated at Eton and at a military academy in the French city of Angers, although he strode like a colossus across the stage of European affairs, Arthur Wellesley was an authentic son of Dublin. Born at Mornington House in Upper Merrion Street in 1769, he did not particularly impress his parents.

When his father, the Earl of Mornington, died, his impoverished mother sent the lad off at the age of eighteen to the army. Against all expectations, young Arthur rose rapidly in the ranks. At the age of twenty-eight he held the rank of colonel and was sent off to India, a highly productive posting, which lasted eight years.

Back in Europe for the Napoleonic alarms, Wellesley continued to perform spectacularly. In 1809 he was made commander-in-chief in the Peninsular War and managed to eject the French from Iberia – in return for which he acquired the title of Duke of Wellington, the rank of field marshal and the handsome sum of £400,000.

What more could he do? The unstoppable Irishman sprang into action when Napoleon escaped from Elba and defeated him roundly at Waterloo, for which deed all of Europe was grateful. Wellington went on to become Prime Minister, which was probably a mistake; like most holders of that office, he eventually fell foul of public opinion.

Dublin's tribute to its famous son was the Wellington Monument, the massive Phoenix Park structure still said to be Europe's highest obelisk. The Duke, for his part, was not an admirer of his native city. When reminded of his origins, he liked to say: 'Being born in a stable doesn't make one a horse.'

The Best Breakfast in Dublin

Smithfield Fruit and Vegetable Market

WEAK, watery light leaks over the eastern horizon into the streets. The city is quiet but not silent. A taxi passes. Two ladies of the night click-clack their way towards the North Circular Road. A man, beyond reach in drink, tries to develop enough momentum to take him up Greek Street.

Even in the early morning Dublin is a city of life – if you know where to look. It's a crossover time. Through the ghost town the fag-end of the night before mingles with the early stirrings of the new day. Nightlife and daylife, one in bleary retreat to bed, the other fresh faced and ready to start. Here in these old streets at this unearthly hour, you'll get the best breakfast in Dublin if you know your way round.

This part of the city has seen some nights and days, some breakfasts down the years. It was always a place of commerce – in food and fish, in horses and the law.

Wall detail at the Smithfield Fruit and Vegetable Market ⸺⸺⸺ 33

The liveliest place in town between five and seven in the morning.

It began to take shape when Strongbow and his high-tech Norman army of bow and mail drove the older Norse out of the little south-bank city. They crossed the Liffey and became our first north-siders, bringing their 'ostman' name to Oxmantown. At the heart of the old north side, St Mary's Abbey was once the richest monastery in all the Pale. It was here that Lambert Simnel came in 1487 for support in his claim to the English throne. Abbot Champfleur, no doubt after a good breakfast, lined his Cistercian house behind the pretender and had him crowned with a diadem from the Abbey's jewel box.

It didn't do him much good.

Fifty years later St Mary's faced dissolution at the hands of Henry VIII. There was just time for the Abbey to make another compelling appearance on history's stage. In 1534 Lord Thomas Fitzgerald led his 140 silken horsemen into St Mary's to declare his revolt against Henry VIII. What a sight Silken Thomas' band must have made! It didn't do him any good either. Three years later, after a last breakfast, he and his uncles were hanged, drawn and quartered at Tyburn. Today all that remains of St Mary's is the rib-vaulted chapter house which contains a reconstruction of one of the cloister arcades.

When John Speed made his Dublin map in 1610 it was still a small city of about 9,000 citizens – '5,459 English and 2,221 Irish,' according to the first census taken in the mid-century. There was one bridge well west of Christ Church.

The north side was a *rus in urbe*, a place of orchards, farms, monastery gardens and decent houses, quite separate from the bigger, rougher south side. Within two generations the Duke of Ormonde had started things rolling – new bridges, wider streets, elegant public buildings – which would bind Dublin north and south into a capital city. For a time the city's commercial life would beat out from Capel Street. Then the centre of gravity moved east when a path was cleared through decaying houses and inns to allow old Drogheda Street to reach the Liffey – eventually becoming our O'Connell Street.

Above: side entrance to the Smithfield market

Breakfast?

Right, just around the corner we find two handsome stone females above a pillared arch. Some 40 feet above the street, they lean on the city's coat of arms. Pass beneath them early enough to a bustling pre-dawn world of men doing deals. We're in the Dublin Corporation Fruit and Vegetable Market, the liveliest place in town between five and seven in the morning. Chefs, hotel catering managers, restaurateurs, shopkeepers, all who need to know that food is fresh make their way here a couple of times a week to prod and squeeze and sniff the bounty coming in from farms and harbours and airports. Clementines from Andalucia, grapefruit from Zimbabwe, iceberg lettuces from the Isle of Ely, pomegranates like mortal sins from Turkey . . . and from all over Ireland good-looking vegetables.

A stroll along the aisles is a geography lesson combined with an orgy for the olfactory organ. Until the 1890s the streets and alleys of the area were cluttered with the stalls and carts of food sellers. It was lively, but it wasn't exactly hygienic. Dublin decided it needed better and in 1892 the new Market, in yellow and red brick with liberal helpings of classical masonry, was opened.

Next door there's a different assault on the nose. Crates of squirming prawn are being auctioned at the Fish Market. 'One twenty? Do I hear one twenty?' roars the man with the pad-and-pen. 'One ten? One ten? No. Yes, I have a pound. I have one ten. One twenty. I have one thirty.' Eyes flash. Eyebrows flicker. Fingers twitch. 'Gone at one thirty.' A deal is done with tiny gestures.

As if of one mind, seventeen men move to encircle three crates of black lobsters. The crates tell of their travels – Killybegs, Dunmore East, Howth, Kilkeel, Milford Haven, Oostende. And their owners. There's some belonging to 'Seán Óg' whoever he may be. A crustacean falls out and a boot accidentally crushes it. 'Like the sound of lawyers' legs breaking,' laughs the boot's proprietor. After merchants of food and fish, this part of Dublin is thick with lawyers on the way to or from the Four Courts. This is a place of aromas, rough and delicate. Tangy salt smells of massed plaice mix with chestnut mushrooms or leather-leaf Costa Rican fern or Spanish megaonions. At the back of them all, however, there is that irresistible scent known to all Dubliners from the cradle – that of the Irish breakfast. At Paddy's Place there's bacon, sausages, fried bread, toast, eggs and mugs of tea.

It's a no-nonsense restaurant tucked up against one wall. Being essentially open to the elements, the Markets can be chilly in the early morning. But Paddy's Place is a snug caboose up against one of the big walls. The perfect place to set yourself up for the journey home.

Arthur Guinness

TRUE DUBS

IT could have been Holyhead. Or Caernarvon. But history decided that Arthur Guinness should set up his brewery in Dublin. This prototype Irish entrepreneur from Celbridge had his first taste of business when he leased a Leixlip brewery in 1756. He was thirty-one. He soon realised that he was dealing in liquid gold.

Excessive drinking was de rigeur in the Ireland of his day. One titled host of a typical Dublin bacchanalia wrote that 'out of pure hospitality and friendliness wine was poured down the guests' throats until they wallowed in filth and beastliness'. And that was the quality! The plain folk preferred whiskey and ale. Young Guinness soon decided that he was bigger than Leixlip. A place across the water would get his ale past the hostile export tariffs designed to protect English brewers. He looked high and low in Wales, but returned home without finding what he wanted. Then, in 1759, he bought 'a brewhouse, two malt houses, some stables and a dwelling house' at St James's Gate from Martin Rainsford, a small brewer – he later became Lord Mayor and a street bearing his name still runs behind the Guinness Hop Store. It was almost twenty years before Arthur Guinness began to brew his black porter. And it was twenty years more before he stopped brewing the ales, which were his first products. St James's Gate was on the way to becoming the biggest brewery in the world.

A resolute man of strong opinions, Guinness was often driven to defend his burgeoning baby. In 1775 a row over water rights led the City Fathers to send a team of workers to cut off the brewery's supply. The master brewer arrived on the scene with a pickaxe. He got his way and the water kept flowing.

Later his black porter faced a popular boycott because of Guinness's deep opposition to the ideals of the United Irishmen. An ever-stronger export business was his answer. Politics and porter were ever a potent mixture in Ireland.

Peerless Piers!

Dún Laoghaire

COMING back to Dún Laoghaire on a car ferry late one summer evening, two boys got themselves as far forward as possible on the top open-air deck. Squeezing between the flapping anoraks of English and Welsh passengers, they were just able to get their chins up on to the wooden rail. 'I see it,' said one. 'There! Look! The white roof.' They were identifying their school, Harold in Glasthule, from a totally new angle. Their light voices rang like bells as they picked off the geography of their little lives – the spires, the harbour walls, the lighthouse, the huge blockhouse of the shopping centre, the Martello at Sandycove, Dalkey Island and, off in the back of the panorama, the stubby obelisk on Killiney Head.

It was clear to adults within earshot that the boys loved their home town. And those seeing it for the first time knew that Dún Laoghaire was indeed a special place.

It's been a special place for quite some time. Laoghaire, one of our High Kings, gave the place its name. He lived in Patrick's century and, according to tradition, ordered a fort in these parts. In De Vesci Gardens, near the old heart of the now-sprawling borough, you'll find Laoghaire's Chair, a large stone sofa which is either the real thing or an eighteenth-century piece of fun.

Not a lot happened in old Dunleary down the centuries. A few fishermen's cottages clustered around a single inn and, half a mile away, creamy church land made Monkstown the envy of these parts. Then came the harbour, the first of a series of quantum leaps which lifted the hamlet out of obscurity.

The surveyors, engineers and stonemasons arrived with their wives and families at Dalkey Hill in 1817. First they built a few rude homes for themselves – they knew it would take a working life to hack enough granite out of the hill, to cut it into shape, to run it down to the sea. It took twenty-five years.

A special small railway was built to move the stone. Its path, now a lovely walk right down to the sea at the People's Park, is still called the Metals because of the metal rails it once carried. The great project had just begun when George IV came calling in 1821. He left from Dunleary and the place was never quite the same – it was renamed Kingstown and so remained until, a century later, the new Irish order decided that old Laoghaire should be reinstated.

View of Dún Laoghaire from the East Pier

The harbour is Dún Laoghaire's monumental treasure. The East Pier, the more popular of the two, is laden with antique furniture. The Boyd obelisk pays discreet homage to Captain J. McNeil Boyd who went down with the *Ajax* and five of his company while trying to save the stricken brig *Neptune* in a storm in Scotsman's Bay in 1861. Further along there's a visitor from the old Nile – a wind gauge which looks like a tomb from ancient Egypt.

At the end the Battery. This fortress built around the lighthouse boasted four large gun emplacements, none ever fired in battle. Today, as in all its 153 years, this is the place to come in order to take in the pleasing perfection of Dun Laoghaire's geography.

The West Pier is longer, less travelled. It's a different experience with its own more solitary charm. In its elbow, you'll see the old lightships which once rode at anchor over hidden sand banks off shore. Now they are adventure centres for the sea scouts.

From the end of either pier it's clear what Dún Laoghaire gets up to when it's not working – it's playing or praying, apparently. Every little jetty within the harbour has its huddle of yachts, some moored, some up in dry dock being scraped or painted. Over by Salthill just on the Dublin side of the harbour there's a newly tarmacked slope leading down to the sea where, whatever the weather, you'll always see a sailboard or two at sea.

Of course, it's a walker's paradise – and could easily become one for cyclists. One of the great walks is to start at Sandycove, march along the promenade at Scotsman's Bay, past the East Pier, pause to ponder Andrew O'Connor's superb bronze Crucifixion which seems to be cherished anew, on past the Italianate Town Hall, on through the interesting masonry of the harbour until you pass the West Pier and reach the old path between the railway and the sea which will bring you to the Martello tower at Seapoint and the terraced villas of Brighton Vale. And you might just spot two elderly residents – a well-known pair of grey herons who take turn to check the rocks for edibles at low tide.

After the harbour, the other great quantum leap was the arrival of the railway. Suddenly Kingstown was accessible to Dubliners. From 1834 they came to visit and they came to stay. New streets and squares of elegant houses were built – and snapped up. The Grand Tour was the done thing at the time, so the whole of Dublin south coast began

to take on Italian names . . . Frescati, Maretimo, Tivoli, Clarinda, Sorrento, Vico and many more.

Church building boomed too. There was much praying to be done in those less secular times. The dominant spire is that of St Michael's, the borough's central Catholic church. Itself a later addition to the original church, the spire is all that survived the fire in 1966. It stands beside the new church.

A little to the east stands the smaller, but much lovelier spire of the Mariner's Church, with its unusual and subtle curved lines. The Mariner's Church now houses the National Maritime Museum, whose opening hours should be checked before making a special journey. Inside is an extraordinary collection of bits and pieces, including several beautiful models, a huge 2-million-candle-power reflecting light which did duty at the Baily for seventy years and a French long boat from Bantry Bay in 1796.

You can't put a foot out in Dún Laoghaire without bumping into history. Treat yourself, if you haven't been there for a while.

Charles Robert Maturin

TRUE DUBS

SILK stockings, a blue coat, a paste of flour covering his mouth and a red wafer of indeterminate feciture stuck to his forehead . . . such was the extraordinary appearance of Charles Robert Maturin when he sat at his writing desk creating one of his famous macabre stories. The Reverend Maturin was a most unusual Dubliner.

As a boy of seven, Maturin would have heard adults about him talk of the dreadful events afflicting the country which had ejected his family a century before. By the time our man arrived on the scene in 1782, the Huguenots had entered confidently into the life of anglophone Dublin. They were only vestigially French, but they were still most definitely Protestant, although many championed Catholic rights. After digesting a full classical education at Trinity College, Maturin went about God's work by way of the Church of Ireland.

After a number of years as a curate in Loughrea, County Galway, he returned to his native city to a living at St Peter's Church.

However, the young priest's heart lay in the arts, particularly in literature of the Gothic genre. Toiling moodily at his writing desk, Maturin produced six novels in all. The one for which he is best remembered is *Melmoth The Wanderer,* a dark tale which borrowed themes from the experience of Huguenot and Jew. The book became something of a bestseller around Europe and in France Honoré de Balzac was so moved that he penned a sequel, *Melmoth Réconcilié.*

Success appears to have made Maturin somewhat eccentric. His home in York Street became the epicentre of outrageous Dublin. He threw dancing parties, often in the afternoon. Visitors reported that the host's salon had been done over with great ottomans, oriental carpets, ceiling paintings of clouds and eagles and walls bearing scenes from his melodramatic novels.

Maturin liked to do his writing in a crowded room. The paste over his mouth prevented him from joining in the gossip. And the red wafer signified that he was in the arms of his muse. He died, bankrupt through his extravagant parties, at the age of 44 in 1824.

6

Spiritual Heart of the City

Christ Church

WHERE is Dublin's spiritual heart? An appropriate point to ponder as we find Christmas upon us once again. A city the size of Dublin has many spiritual hearts, many places which speak deeply and usually silently to its people. Indoor or outdoor, sacred or secular, there can be few places in all of Dublin with the mystical power of the crypt of Christ Church. Stand here on the dusty floor among the repeating arches and be quiet. In the bleak artificial light you're looking at the work of men who planted a great city at this place in a small, divided town a long time ago.

When Richard de Clare captured Dublin in murderous violence in 1170 an early priority was a substantial physical statement of Norman power. An imposing place of worship was the logical thing so Strongbow ordered in the masons and heavers to erect a cathedral on this rise on the south banks of the Liffey. The fact that the site was already occupied by a church wasn't about to stop the new master of Dublin.

The wooden Church of the Holy Trinity had been the centre of the fortified town for 132 years. It had been erected in 1038 by Donatus, Dublin's first bishop and an Irishman. The land was provided by none other than the long-lived Sitric of the Silk Beard, the last Viking king of Dublin. Sitric had just returned from a pilgrimage to Rome but, as they say, it was far from it he was reared. Like most powerful men of the day, Sitric was no stranger to war and trouble. His earlier years had been one long catalogue of battle and siege and hostage taking. And then there was Clontarf.

Half a lifetime ago he had made another pilgrimage – to the Isle of Man to seek help against a man who would be the Irish King. The warlord Brodar came to help and, it's said, destiny led him to the tent of Brian Boru at the end of that long bloody Good Friday in 1014. They fought. Brodar lost his legs. Brian lost his life. Strongbow shoved over the little wooden church to make room for the new stone structure to be built by the best available hands. Six years later he was dead, but not before a few more rounds of bloodletting. Is he still at Christ Church? Popular lore places him inside the effigy of an armoured knight which stands under a south bay of the nave. Beside it is a shorter figure which, some say, is Strongbow's son who was foolish enough to show his fear of battle. The tyrant killed the boy, they say, and chopped him in two as a warning to others. Fanciful probably, although it seems highly likely that Strongbow would have been buried at the cathedral he commissioned. Sadly, it's believed that the large effigy dates from the fourteenth century, although the smaller figure may be a fragment of the original. None of this got in the way of an old Dublin tradition of nominating 'Strongbow's Tomb' as the place for the payment of debts.

If there is doubt about Strongbow's precise location, there can be little about that of St Laurence O'Toole. This Leinster nobleman became Dublin's first archbishop in 1162 and eight years later he was chosen to deal with Strongbow when the Normans surrounded the city. Laurence is a somewhat tragic figure of the period. A realist, he recognised the overwhelming skills of the newcomers – their sword and mail and skill of organisation ran rings around both Irish and Norse. He worked for a rational peace, but Henry II played cat and mouse with him and refused to let him sail for Ireland from an English port.

The frustrated prelate tried to get home by way of France, but died en route at an Augustinian house at Eu in Normandy. Only his heart came back to his cathedral on the hill by the Liffey. It's there still, in a metal casket hanging on a wall not far from the spot where the man who changed his life might, or might not, lie. Laurence's Augustinians ran the cathedral down the turbulent centuries until England split with Rome over Henry VIII's reproductive troubles. The Dissolution in 1541 saw Christ Church pass to a dean and chapter.

Until 1871 British Crown officers came here to be formally invested. Today it's the seat of the Anglican Bishop of Dublin and Glendalough and the Metropolitan Cathedral of the Southern province of the Church of Ireland. Like any building with mileage, Christ Church is a riot of styles and times with some pieces of the original surviving. Along with St Patrick's, however, it suffered at the hands of well-meaning Victorian fools who indulged in large-scale reconstructions of Dublin's two old cathedrals. The great sin was the demolition of the Long Choir of St John de Paul, built in 1358. Apart from that, large swathes of the original walls were entombed behind new masonry. They did leave the original Romanesque door as they found it.

We should be grateful that they didn't get around to giving the crypt a once-over. You feel the chill as soon as you descend the stone staircase. Once it was used for prayer. Then it filled with less pious life when shopkeepers were allowed to do business down here. Then it began to take the dead, among them a cat and a mouse who got stuck in the organ. They died, apparently in mid-chase, and now lie mummified in a glass case in the crypt. There's no sign of the soldier who wandered unwisely down a dark passage during the funeral of an eighteenth-century general. He was found dead weeks afterwards. The passage is now bricked up.

Yes, a place with mileage.

The distinctive bridge and synod hall at Christ Church

James Clarence Mangan

TRUE DUBS

'O my dark Rosaleen, do not sigh, do not weep . . .' The plaintive words were hammered into the heads of generations of Irish schoolchildren by teachers imbued with bursting pride in the new Ireland, even if the nation was only partly formed. Throughout their lives the children can, if they so choose, dip into their memory to retrieve the haunting words – and try to haul more words back from the past.

'My Dark Rosaleen' is the poem for which James Clarence Mangan is best remembered. In fact, the allegory in which poor, put-upon Ireland is represented by a distressed young woman was based upon 'Roisín Dubh', a poem in Irish dating from the era of the last great Gaelic leaders in the late sixteenth century.

Mangan was born into poverty in Dublin's Fishamble Street in 1803. After forty-six years of strenuous effort he died in poverty not far away – in the Meath Hospital, of cholera and general malnutrition. His melancholy eloquence had not provided him with a sustainable life.

It was after ten years' slaving in a mean scrivener's office that the lonely young man of twenty-five years finally decided to try his hand at writing for a living. He got the odd piece into the magazines of the day, but hardly enough to keep him. Sympathetic friends and admirers got him occasional employment in Trinity College's great library and at the Ordnance Survey.

His gift with words allowed him to learn French, German, Spanish and Latin – but never Irish. Eugene O'Curry, the great self-taught scholar who also worked in the Ordnance Survey, introduced him to 'Roisín Dubh' and, it's believed, provided him with a working translation. It was from this that Mangan built his majestic and moving version.

A Treasure full of Treasures!

Phoenix Park

IT'S the straightest two and a half miles in Dublin. From Parkgate to Castleknock, the main road runs through the Phoenix Park like a knife through butter. Dubliners like to claim that these 1,752 acres constitute the largest city park in Europe. Is the Bois de Boulogne at 2,100 acres not part of Paris? Size isn't everything. Dublin's Phoenix Park is certainly big enough and it's overflowing with treasures big and small, dead and alive. The living treasure is the herd of fallow deer now well into its fourth century.

They can usually be spotted in the Fifteen Acres, that municipal prairie which can swallow half a dozen games of hurling and football and still leave plenty of room for the model aeroplane men. Sometimes, if the grass is greener, the deer will cross the main road to the White Fields over by the Ashtown Gate. Silently, timidly, these members of a graceful animal nation lay daily claim to the open meadows where their progenitors were brought in 1662 by the first Duke of Ormonde.

Chesterfield Avenue, which runs through the centre of the Phoenix Park

James Butler got his Irish title for being a faithful royalist. He had worked assiduously through the decade of Cromwell for the restoration of Charles II in 1660 and for reward was given Ireland. In the past he had done the king's work against the Irish. As Lord Lieutenant, Ormonde moved into 'The Phoenix', a royal mansion on Thomas Hill on the north side of the Liffey where the Magazine Fort would later be built. Previous occupants had been Strafford and Henry Cromwell. All about was royal land, wide acres which Henry VIII had grabbed from the Knights Hospitallers at the Dissolution of the Monasteries a century earlier.

From his vantage point above the Liffey, Ormonde looked at the rolling acres and concluded that they should make a deer park fit for a king – and a king's deputy. But when he brought in the first fallow deer he was starting a deer park fit for a people. When it was reported that venison was beginning to appear in the diet of plain unprivileged folk in the district, the Lord Lieutenant ordered a perimeter wall. The contract, worth £6,000, went to James Dodson but his wall 'did a Jericho' in several places and had to be rebuilt within a few years.

It was almost a century before the Phoenix Park was opened to the public. In 1745 Philip Dormer Stanhope, the Earl of Chesterfield, arrived to run Ireland. And Ireland was pleasantly surprised – he was progressive, friendly and quite indifferent to a person's religion. Within two years of his arrival, Chesterfield had eased conditions for

Catholics and allowed the building of several churches.

He seems to have marked out the Phoenix Park for his personal interest. New paths were installed. Thousands of trees were planted. Sylvan promenades were laid out with sunhouses and bandstands where military music was played on summer evenings. A new central avenue was stretched from the south-east to the north-west. It was called Chesterfield Avenue and the eponymous peer dipped into his own bottomless pocket to erect the graceful Phoenix Column which has just reclaimed its place at the road's halfway point. The Park as we know it was starting to take shape. A few decades after Chesterfield's time, in 1781, the Viceregal Lodge was established at the rather plain abode of one Robert Clements. It wasn't long before the simple brick had been covered and the building began to acquire the classical additions judged necessary for the health and happiness of 'all gentlefolk of condition'.

Not in their worst nightmares would the wigged and powdered residents of the Viceregal Lodge have foreseen the days of Áras an Uachtaráin and their replacement by people such as Douglas Hyde, Éamon de Valera and Mary Robinson.

Down the years the Park has always reflected the current concerns of the country. The nineteenth century had roared into life with Napoleon striding all over Europe to meet his comeuppance at the hands of an Irishman. A few years later, after much stumbling and argument, the 205-foot Wellington Monument took triumphal shape in a triangular piece of parkland down by Parkgate. And to this day people wonder how those young fellows managed to climb up so high.

With France defeated, the Anglocentric world of which Ireland was a part settled into its mercantile-scientific stride. The Park became the site of the world's second zoo in 1830, just two years after London. In its first year about 30,000 people made the journey out from the city to see the animals, the main attraction being a lioness about to produce cubs. Can you do the Park in a day? By car or bicycle, you certainly can. On foot? Yes, if you plan it properly. A circuit of the perimeter roads is between 6 and 7 miles, no more than a morning's work for the dedicated walker. The serpentine road along the Park's southern flank will warm you up nicely. It takes you from Parkgate or the Islandbridge Gate west past the Chapelizod Gate and St Mary's Hospital to the Furry Glen and the lovely Knockmaroon Gate. Pop into the Information and Nature Centre here if it's open.

The northern rim of the Park is considerably shorter. Here you'll find the OPW interpretive centre, which is well worth a visit. The road moves on behind Áras an Uachtaráin until it separates the Zoo from Garda Headquarters and finally decants you back at Parkgate. The Park, whether its name derives from a spring of '*fionn uisce*' or a fiery, winged legend, is one of the reasons why Dublin is a very special place.

Stags resting near Áras an Uachtaráin, Phoenix Park

Henry Grattan

TRUE DUBS

'*MON père est le plus grand homme en Irlande*,' Mary Grattan used to tell her classmates. The headmistress, Madame Terson, insisted on French being spoken whenever possible by the girls at the Huguenot School in Clontarf. She had an excellent reputation and Henry Grattan was happy to have his daughter in her hands.

It was in 1775 that the 29-year-old lawyer first appeared on the floor of the parliament on College Green, which would take his name. Grattan spoke eloquently and effectively for fair play for Irish trade. Soon he moved on to legislative independence for the country – and freedom for Ireland's Catholics.

Sadly, London was not interested in such matters. It was a bitter irony for men such as Henry Grattan that, as France hurled out intoxicating ideas of freedom and human rights, England was tightening its grip on Ireland. Bribery and threat were freely used to persuade the Irish Parliament to sign its own death certificate.

Grattan was fifty-four when the Act of Union was passed. Poor health had persuaded him to quit his seat in 1797 but a year later he returned to the House to fight the Union.

Failure sent him into retirement to Tinnehinch, County Wicklow – for five years. In 1805 he took a Dublin seat in the English Commons, demanding freedom for Catholics, autonomy for Ireland and other undeniable rights.

At the age of seventy-four Henry Grattan was still travelling to London to speak up for freedom. He died there in 1820, after travelling by canal barge from Liverpool. He is buried at Westminster Abbey.

8

Inner City of Knowledge!

Trinity College

TYSON is loitering in the shrubbery by the Berkeley Library, no doubt hoping to tear the head off a morning robin. His orange livery and substantial size make success unlikely but hope springs eternal in the feline breast.

Trinity's maintenance staff gave Tyson his name – and each morning they put out a saucer of milk for him. He's been around for four or five years, undisputed king of the college's resident feral cats. Cats have been living comfortable lives in and around Trinity right down its 400 years. And before the university, Tyson's forebears grew fat on Augustinian pickings.

The Priory of All Hallows had been established on unwanted swampy land east of the medieval city. Between it and the walls up at Dublin Castle was its companion Nunnery of St Mary de Hogges and open commonage watered by the River Stein.

The monks and the nuns were scattered by Henry VIII's Dissolution of Monasteries between 1534 and 1539 and about fifty years later Trinity came into existence. The avowed purpose of the new college was to provide Ireland with an engine of Protestantism as 'a counter blast to Popery'. Trinity would provide an elite of privileged young men trained in the Protestant way of thinking.

Around the main quadrangle of red brick were gathered hall, chapel, kitchen and buttery. Trinity's four fellows provided between them three lectures a day. Afternoons were usually passed in attempts at learned discussions on fine points of divinity – conducted, of course, in Latin. None of these early buildings remains today. Nor does the virulent Protestantism which marked Trinity's origins. In the generations that followed the first students were many who would champion the cause of religious freedom for their Catholic neighbours.

Dublin's axis moved east towards the sea in the following centuries. Sackville Street replaced Capel Street as the commercial heart of the city. Trinity, always walled and separate, was surrounded and absorbed by new streets. It became that splendid thing, a city of knowledge within a city of life.

There is nothing more calming than to walk through the arched entrance on College Green, cross the wooden hexagonal tiles and enter the cobbled square within. There facing you is the Campanile, where the high altar of the Augustinians once stood. So many have gone this way. James Ussher was one of Trinity's first students. Oliver

It's surprising how many Dubliners have not been to see the Book of Kells

Goldsmith earned his education by cleaning the quadrangle and carrying food up to the fellows' hall. Jonathan Swift arrived at the age of fifteen, stayed seven undistinguished years and got a degree only because of a special dispensation. The Provost under whom Swift laboured was the irrepressible Narcissus Marsh. An Englishman, he was identified by the Duke of Ormonde as a substantial thinker of integrity and a believer in the rights of Protestant man.

Marsh wore his considerable learning like pearls rather than chains. A great linguist, he placed Irish on Trinity's curriculum. He went on to become Archbishop of Dublin and established Marsh's Library beside St Patrick's Cathedral.

The west front, so familiar with its blue clock observing the length of Dame Street, was completed in 1759 just as Henry Grattan was arriving to hone his considerable conscience. The splendid Provost's House was finished the same year.

Trinity's place in the life of the city had its darker side. In the eighteenth and nineteenth centuries gowned students were greatly feared and reviled in certain quarters. In 1734 a junior dean, Edward Ford, was murdered by the students. Woundings, mutilations and other outrages were common enough.

The guilds of the city were at this time from one or other of the two religious camps. The butchers of Ormonde Market were Catholic, while the weavers of the Liberties were Protestant. They often did brutal battle, the Trinity students working with the weavers. It is recorded that, after one particularly rough brawl, several students ended their lives strung up on butchers' hooks.

One large reason to visit Trinity is, of course, the Book of Kells. It's surprising how many Dubliners have not been to see this priceless treasure created around about 1,200 years ago by the Columban monks of Iona. It is believed that the astonishing work of inscribing and engraving was perhaps begun on the Scottish isle but finally accomplished at the Meath monastery. It was stolen in Kells in 1007, presumably for the bejewelled shrine which enclosed it, because the book itself was found 'under a sod' and returned to its home. It arrived in Dublin in 1654 – sent for safekeeping during the Cromwellian disturbances by Bishop Henry Jones of Meath. So it arrived at Trinity where it has remained in safe hands.

Now it resides in a cool, dark chamber beneath the Long Room, the great arched library with dusty books reaching high up into the ceiling. On discreet display here is another great book which Trinity

The Campanile (bell tower)

acquired just a few years ago: the first printed book in the Irish language. The little alphabet and catechism was made in 1571, twenty years before All Hallows would become Trinity.

No doubt whoever was caretaking the premises at the time was putting out a daily saucer of milk for Tyson's forebears.

Bram Stoker

TRUE DUBS

SOME blamed it on a plate of crab, taken after a particularly lugubrious journey by carriage across the Scottish Highlands. Like much about the Dubliner who wrote the most successful novel in the genre of Gothic horror, it's probably an apocryphal tale.

Abraham Stoker was born on 8 November 1847, the year in which the potato famine reached its height. Dreadful tales of death and disease swept the land, but the Stokers were largely immune from the disaster. Professional folk of the Protestant persuasion, they had a fine home at 15, Marino Crescent. Although the theatre was Bram Stoker's great love, he obediently entered the civil service after his Trinity education. While working for the state, he pestered the *Evening Mail* with reviews of plays. The paper was impressed enough to publish some of them, but not impressed enough to pay the young critic.

He was almost thirty years of age and living in Harcourt Street when Henry Irving burst upon his life. The great actor came to Dublin to regale the city with some of his Shakespearean interpretations in the autumn of 1876. Stoker was immediately transfixed and remained in this state, almost to the point of slavery, for the rest of his life.

The Dubliner became Irving's manager in 1878 and remained in the position until the actor died in 1905. Along the way Stoker found time to do his own writing: twelve novels of which only *Dracula* is remembered today. The bloodsucking count from beyond the Carpathians was an extraordinary creation, even if it owes its existence to various sources ... there was Vlad the Impaler, the brutal medieval protector of Transylvania; there was *Carmilla*, another vampire story created by Sheridan Le Fanu, another Dubliner; and there was that meal of Scottish crab on a dark night in the Highlands while in the abject service of a great Victorian actor.

Bram Stoker died in 1912 after seven lonely years without Irving. His wife and only son mourned dutifully – they knew who had been the most important person in the life just ended.

9

The view of views of the old town!

Killiney Hill

WHERE can the serious Dub get the best view of the old town? The top of Howth Head would seem like a sensible first thought. Three Rock Mountain makes a lot of sense too. However, Killiney Hill may just be the perfect belvedere because it's both low enough and high enough to register the great sweep of the panorama – and it gives you Howth in all its ancient indolence.

The geography of the promontory at the southern end of Dublin Bay's great crescent is a very feminine thing indeed – like much else about Dublin. It's three hills are gentle and covered. Unlike Howth, they don't demand to be tramped and touched. But those who hear their subtler call will be well rewarded. These parts, now so elegant and civilised, were once almost as dangerous as Clontarf's notorious Mud Island. Before the railway drew monied Dubliners to live by the lovely coast around Dalkey and Killiney, this was a haunt of lawless men.

Many of the little inlets which ran from old Dunleary to what would become Sorrento Point were hideaways for pirates who preyed on the vessels heading for old Coliemore Harbour or all the way up the dangerous sea road to Dublin. James McKinley and Thomas Gidley were two such gentlemen. In 1765 they were part of a piratical gang who boarded the *Sandwich* off the coast and murdered its captain and several passengers. A year later the two were executed and their bodies hung in chains out on the Muglins, the rocky stragglers north-east of Dalkey Island. Not an unusual sight in those days. The powers that were took particular exception to lawlessness in these parts because the Lord Lieutenant, Lord Deputies and Viceroys often came this way. Before the railways, before the huge new harbour at Dunleary, before the district was Italianised, the powerful came and went from little Coliemore.

In those days Dalkey Hill – or Telegraph Hill as some still call it because of the old semaphore station on top – was considerably bulkier. It lost much of its granite substance when Dún Laoghaire's immense two-pier harbour was built 150 years ago. It lost a bit more during the boom in local mansion-making which the railway triggered. William Dargan's first Irish railway had stopped at Kingstown station in 1834 – after a twenty-minute trip from

The view towards Bray from Killiney Hill

Westland Row. Ten years later Dalkey had its own extension from Kingstown – the famous Atmospheric Railway!

Samuel Clegg was an adept of hydraulics. His grip of the theories of gravity and the vacuum was second to none. He whipped up enough support for a railway which would suck trains up the hill to Dalkey by means of a giant straw laid between the tracks. Gravity would return the trains to Kingstown. And it worked – initially.

However, problems mounted with the elaborate and impractical valve of leather, tallow and iron which allowed the train to convert the vacuum into movement. By 1854, despite the enthusiasm of all sorts of people, including Isambard Kingdom Brunel and several French

Unlike Howth they don't demand to be tramped and touched

rail experts, the Atmospheric Railway gave way to conventional steam. The circuit of Dalkey Hill can be done either way. With an eye to walking the three hills, the car park on the landward side is the ideal starting point. Through the shrubbery are tracks into the delightful quarries under the old signal house.

Up the man-made cliffs you go by way of the staircase. At the top turn left and follow your nose – if you can take your eyes off the sublime view that revolves as you go. The track leads down to Torca Road where George Bernard Shaw summered happily as a youngster at the cottage of George Vandeleur Lee, his mother's singing teacher. Turn right towards Bray and soon you find yourself high and airy above Vico and Killiney Beach. Now the choice is yours – back to the car park or up Killiney Hill.

More wooded at first, but at the top is the view of views. The obelisk, very satisfactory from a distance, is coarse enough at close quarters. It was erected by John Mapas, master of Killiney Castle 250 years ago, as relief work for the local poor after a fearful winter. 'Last year being hard with the poor,' states a plaque on the north face, 'the walls about these hills and this etc erected by John Mapas, Esq. June 1742.'

The view of Dalkey Island from Killiney Hill

A century later Robert Warren mentioned his repairs in stone. Sadly there's no sign of the staircase and viewing platform which Mapas had provided.

It's still an overwhelming 360-degree view from Howth, past the city, over to the huge chimney of the old lead mines on Carrickgollogan and the Dublin Mountains, down to Djouce, the Sugarloaf, Bray Head, the open sea and back to Dalkey Island below. To the southwest there's Mullins' Hill – or Roches Hill – the smallest and least memorable of the three. However, it's there and that's reason enough to finish the job.

Patrick Sarsfield

TRUE DUBS

OH, that this were for Ireland . . . the dying words of the first Lord Lucan as he watched his blood flow from him on the field of Landen between Liege and Louvain in July 1693. The great Irish general gave his life for France, for the colossal ambitions of Louis XIV against his various and mostly Protestant neighbours to the east. Patrick Sarsfield earned his earldom from another Catholic king, but James II was as great a failure as the Sun King was a success.

A privileged Dubliner, Sarsfield had an annual income of £2,000. He had enjoyed a gentleman's education at a French military school and found himself in the English Life Guards when James II succeeded Charles II. He immediately placed himself at the new monarch's disposal and the Irishman's bravery and strategic imagination were noted at the Battle of Sedgemoor in 1685.

When James II brought the religious war to Ireland, Sarsfield came home and was always in the thick of the action. He masterminded the clearing of the Williamites from Connacht, then went east to see his side routed at the Boyne. During the defence of Limerick, he organised the brilliant ambush of an enemy supply train at Ballyneety aided by the invaluable local knowledge of the raparree, Galloping Hogan.

A year later Sarsfield, now bearing his title, was back in Limerick after the 'dread disaster' at Aughrim. The Jacobite forces knew they were defeated and signed the Treaty of Limerick in 1691. This marked the end of James's hopes of a Catholic restoration in England. It also marked the end of a way of life for Ireland.

It was the year of the Wild Geese. Patrick Sarsfield and about 11,000 other fighting men left Ireland forever to fight and die for France. Two years later the Earl of Lucan watched his life drain away in a place two seas away from home.

10

Brian Boru, the Knights and all that Bull!

Clontarf

BULL is in the nature of Clontarf. Somewhere, in the distant past, between the northern banks of the Liffey estuary and the isthmus that led out to Howth, bulls were kept in the meadows of some lord or abbot. Or, more fancifully, *Cluain Tarbh* took its name from the bull-like roar of the waves charging in off the bay.

Clontarf's borders, like the origin of its name, have long been open to debate. Nowadays Dubliners are in broad agreement that it starts at the double arches of the stone railway bridge. Where it ends is another matter: is it at the wooden bridge to the Bull Island or does it include Dollymount and reach the new Causeway? And does it matter? What does matter is that Clontarf is a most agreeable part of Dublin and has been for quite a few generations.

Outsiders express amazement when they happen upon the shady peace of tree-lined Kincora Road, or the elegant Seafield Road running from the delightful St John's Church of Ireland right down to the sea,

Clontarf's borders, like the origin of its name, have long been open to debate.

or the lively and bracing seafront road where grand Victorian villas and terraces alternate with modern housing giving no particular offence. And the city centre just 3 or 4 miles away.

This was once Templar land. Then 'the Poor Knights of Christ and the Temple of Solomon' got too rich for their own good. They were suppressed most bloodily in France in 1312 on trumped-up charges of profaning crucifixes, worshipping Satan, murdering children and general debauchery. So it was that the vast Templar wealth throughout Christendom, including Clontarf, passed to their rivals, the Knights of the Hospital of St John.

Before the Templars, before the First Crusade set off for Jerusalem with its rallying cry, '*Hierosylem ist perdita,*' contracted to the handier acronym, 'Hip, Hip, Hooray,' Clontarf was the general scene of a long and infamous day's carnage. The fighting ranged over the northern bay to the riverbank opposite little fortified Dubh Linn where Norse and Irish mixed.

The Viking explained away Good Friday 1014, in supernatural terms. Their later accounts spoke of strange signs – axes and swords fighting among themselves, skulls found draped in entrails, hot blood raining down from the heavens. How could man stand against such things? For their part the descendants of Brian Boru, who died with the sword of Brodar of the Isle of Man in his head, wove a national war against the foreigner out of a 'land-grapping' battle between Munster men and Leinster men. In fact, the Norse fought on both sides.

One of Brian's allies was, in fact, Ospak of the Northern Isles. King Sitric of Dublin had voyaged to the Orkneys to enlist his help in the looming showdown, offering his mother by way of a bribe. Ospak, being clearly unimpressed by the ageing and much-bartered Gormflaith, joined Brian.

Over 800 years later a cast-iron door was erected in a wall on Castle Avenue bearing these words: 'Erected over Brian Boroimh's Well by subscription – AD 1860.' There is no particular reason to believe or disbelieve the claim. The intervening eight centuries had transformed the Meadow of the Bulls. Throughout the medieval period and into early modern times, Clontarf remained quite separate from Dublin. Not surprisingly, since on its townward fringe somewhere opposite today's Fairview and East Wall was the appalling Mud Island.

It is said that three brothers dispossessed by the Ulster Plantation settled on this hump of mean, swampy land which was cut off at high tide. Soon other unfortunates joined them and Mud Island began to take on its dreadful character.

Nothing and nobody was safe in this place. The forces of law and order gave it a wide berth even long after it had become part of the mainland. It was a haven of free-roaming killers, thieves and smugglers. Adding to the hellish character of 'the Island' was the presence of victims of disease and deformities who had been driven out of what passed for civilised society. East of Mud Island, the waters of the bay washed a shore which few would recognise today. The sea swept by old Clontarf Island, a low gravel deposit long vanished from the scene, and on to a coast where Fairview Park now stands.

Beyond were the renowned oyster beds just above the anchorage of 'the Quarantine Sloop' on which the authorities detained sailors who looked like they might be carrying something deadly. And beyond the oysters beds, the heart of old Clontarf, the little fishing hamlet and 'the Sheds' where the fish were cured between Vernon Avenue and Conquer Hill.

As times grew safer, Clontarf became a place of big houses and green lanes. The Vernons, who had arrived in the seventeenth century, were the old hands and had a number of residences. The name Dollymount was originally applied by a Vernon to a house in the area – Dolly was his wife, Dorothy.

The rush of Victorian expansion finally made Clontarf a part

Knights Bar | Reception

Indigo Lounge | Conference & Banqueting

Fahrenheit
Grill

of the city. The seafront was transformed and, inland, a prototype suburbia began to form. During this period the area acquired its reputation for happy religious relations – so much so that Protestants elsewhere in Dublin referred to their Clontarf brethern as 'Roman Protestants'. During this period Clontarf's most influential resident was Baron Ardilaun, the philanthropist who gave so much to Dublin. His greatest gift to the city was St Stephen's Green but he also funded the vital restoration of Marsh's Library and an important extension to the Coombe Hospital.

Born Arthur Edward Guinness at St Anne's in 1840, he headed the family firm for ten years until 1877. His estate, still the biggest piece of greenery touching Dublin Bay, was an extraordinary place in its heyday. At the centre was a great Palladian mansion at the end of a long yew-flanked avenue. Spread out before it were the manicured parklands crossed by an ancient right-of-way. Ardilaun arranged for it to be sunken so that the Arcadian view might not be disturbed by passing plain folk.

Over to the west on a shady embankment was the dogs' cemetery where headstones recalled the day 'Tiberius Caesar fell asleep' or the night 'Nero closed his eyes' or simply 'Dear Brutus'. Behind the house was a paradise of woodland tracks and hidden glades with all tracks leading down to the lake by which flowed the little Nanniken on its way to the sea.

Between the wars St Anne's passed into official hands. During the Second World War and in the years of shortage after it, vast ricks of turf were lined up along the avenue. About this time the house burned down accidentally. Much of St Anne's splendour survives today in the capable care of the city.

Cathal Brugha

TRUE DUBS

HE took two days to die. Cathal Brugha had suffered mortal wounds in the intense fighting for O'Connell Street in the opening days of the Civil War. For eight days the battle had raged between the Free Staters and the IRA. Sixty people were dead and over 300 injured. The IRA surrendered. Brugha refused to do so and joined the dead of O'Connell Street.

Born into Dublin's merchant circle at Richmond Avenue in 1874, Charles William St John Burgess was moving through a typical middle-class Catholic education when the Burgess family business collapsed. He was sixteen at the time, a senior pupil at Belvedere College. Family connections were able to get him a position as a clerk in a firm of ecclesiastical suppliers.

For a decade national turmoil provided fertile soil for his republican ideas. By 1899, at the age of twenty-five, he was in the Gaelic League and using the Irish form of his name. As the political temperature rose, so did Brugha's view of the state of Ireland. Like many other like-minded young men, he became convinced that the national question needed settling by force of arms.

By 1913 Brugha, now a businessman and a rebel, was coming up to his fortieth birthday. His early connections with church business had led him to become involved in a firm of chandlers. He was also a lieutenant in the Volunteers. Three years later when Dublin erupted in flames and gunfire, Brugha was high in the inner circle of the IRA. As second in command in the South Dublin Ward, he suffered injuries that left him lame for the few years left to him.

The juggernaut of national affairs roared through his life for six more years. After the Rising he became chief of staff of the IRA and then Minister of Defence. He presided over the first session of the Dáil in 1919. The Civil War placed him behind a gun once again in a battle that would finally see a street bearing his name.

In the folds of the foothills

The Dublin Mountains

HE probably spent his childhood in one of the little valleys of the Dublin Mountains. As he grew to manhood, Dannall Grumbly might have joined in the tavern talk and the table talk of the times, talk of the nasty French and their dangerous ambitions, of the recurring famines of the day, of bitterness and greed as the old Irish lands were redistributed.

The Wild Geese, the fighting strength of Catholic Ireland, had already flown to France and Spain when he was born in 1698. That year 14 per cent of Irish land was held by Catholics. By the time he was sixteen the figure was down to 7 per cent. Master Grumbly, we presume, lived his life around Kiltiernan, Kilmashogue and the Scalp while Jonathan Swift railed against poverty and injustice in Dublin and Johann Sebastian Bach built musical cathedrals in Leipzig. We know nothing about him except that he 'Departed This Life Aged 60 Years In The Year 1758'. Maybe the headstone has his name wrong. Was Dannall a phonetic attempt at Daniel by a semi-literate

Winding roads near Tibradden mountain

Dannall Grumbly's headstone

stonemason? Today he still lies where they laid him along with a score of other now-forgotten farmers, soldiers and landowners in a neatly kept cemetery around a ruined church on Bishop's Lane in Kiltiernan. The little graveyard is typical of County Dublin's ragged southern fringe. In the folds of the foothills are many 'spots' known only to those tenacious enough to root them out.

The border with Wicklow runs out from Bray, right up the middle of the Scalp, across to the easy peaks of Prince William's Seat and Glendoo, down to the summits of Kippure and Seefingan, north to Corrig and then out to the river lowlands. It's a region rich in unnecessary roads, the legacy of mean times when land-grappers needed military protection from the magnificent menace to the south. The Wicklow wilderness was the mountain lair of the dispossessed

> It's a region rich in unnecessary
> roads and the legacy of mean times.

or of others who would be land-grappers. Strongbow and Dermot McMurrough came this way up from the south in the summer of 1170. Their path brought them over the mountains to Glendalough, Glencree and down past the hill that would later be topped by the Hell Fire Club to the plain of Rathfarnham. The Normans achieved only half a conquest. The septs of Wicklow were never subdued and their fighting men were greatly feared, whether mounted or on foot. Toughened by steep lives, they struck at the city with speed, coming out of their mountains down through the foothills, picking off outlying farms and hamlets with ease.

On Easter Monday 1209, just a generation after the new order had installed itself in Dublin, the O'Tooles and O'Byrnes erupted out of the mountains and spilled the blood of about 500 settlers gathered for a day's hurling and trading at Ranelagh, then called Cullenswood. The city of Bristol soon sent more settlers whose seed spoke for centuries of Black Monday.

The septs came again and again – and the Normans often went to meet them, clattering with their armour and broadswords out through the Scalp and over the Featherbeds on the long road to

Glenmacnass and Glenmalure. The Irish almost always won. The flight path of the septs was through Glenasmole or Tibradden, or down off Two Rock and Three Rock. So life hereabouts always had something of the dangerous frontier about it. The dykes and ditches of the Pale gave it a wide berth, keeping well to the north in lowland safety.

One of the south county's most interesting and visible works of man is the great granite chimney built in the early nineteenth century on a spur of Carrickgollogan, the hill which Dubliners call Katty Gollagher. It stands as solidly as ever with just a few steps missing from the spiral staircase around the outside. A mile below at the hill's northern base were the Ballycorus Lead Works, where local ore was smelted to produce lead, some silver and shot. Between the works and the chimney was the flue, an extraordinary serpentine structure that climbed the hill to carry the fumes and the poisons up and away. If you're tenacious enough you can follow the flue up the hill. If you're foolish enough, you can even enter it here and there where the roof has collapsed. The chimney itself is easily reached and well worth the small trek involved.

Across to the west are the bouldered summits of Two Rock and Three Rock and west again is Montpelier topped by the other great visible structure of the Dublin Mountains: the Hell Fire Club sits like a petrified bivouac on the bald hilltop. Built as a shooting lodge in 1725 by William Conolly, Speaker of the Irish Commons and Lord of Castletown, it was a shooting lodge to which the Hell Fire Club often repaired for the purposes of gambling, drinking and fornication – usually when things had become too hot for these rich brats at the Eagle Tavern on Cork Hill.

Older shenanigans took place, according to legend, in Glenasmole, where the Dodder rises. It's difficult to believe that this place with its remarkably sequestered atmosphere lies within 2 miles of rampant suburbia. This most locked-in of Dublin's valleys, which remained Irish-speaking up to the early nineteenth century, had an honourable place in the old sagas of the Fianna. One tale tells of Finn himself coming here with his hounds, Brann and Sceolan, to hunt deer. Instead, the god-man is bewitched by a devil-woman and her Amazons.

It takes three days but all ends well for the heroes in the Valley of the Thrushes. Glenasmole is a little world but it has many 'spots' which, if the day is right, could not be bettered for a quiet read and a sandwich. A stroll along the filter beds of the upper reservoir is therapy itself. It's one of two little lakes produced by the Dodder and its many feeders as they pour down off Kippure.

Never let anybody tell you Dublin is a flat county.

Sinéad de Valera

TRUE DUBS

AT 5 feet 4 inches she wasn't exceptionally small, but beside her towering husband she was nothing less than petite. Not that the Irish public often saw Éamon de Valera and his wife side by side. From the early days of their marriage she devoted herself to home and hearth, while Dev went about the business of nation building.

Sinéad Flanagan was a Balbriggan girl, born in the summer of 1878 and raised at a time when nationalist ideas were running ever more strongly through the towns and hamlets of the north county. There was much learning to be done – and much teaching. She became a teacher and, as the century drew to a close, young red-haired Miss Flanagan found herself in charge of a class of youngsters in a primary school in Dorset Street. Like most nationalists, she believed that the Irish language was a key to nationhood. So in her free time she walked the few hundred yards to Parnell Square, to the Gaelic League's Leinster College, to teach it.

Like other spirited young women of the time, Sinéad Flanagan enjoyed amateur dramatics. She once chatted with the novelist George Moore about whether or not she could manage a stage career. It appears that he advised against it. In 1908 she was still teaching Irish in Parnell Square when a strikingly tall lecturer in mathematics joined the movement and began to attend her Irish classes. Two years later she married Éamon de Valera. As revolutionary affairs absorbed her husband, Sinéad was increasingly occupied with the family. The children began to arrive. Then, when they were six years married, the Easter Rising.

The years after 1916 were difficult and often lonely for Sinéad de Valera. Her husband was behind bars in Dartmoor or Maidstone or Lincoln – or away in the United States – while she raised their children, now four in number. In 1920 Dev was in America raising support for the new Republic. Sinn Féin managed to produce a false passport for Sinéad to visit him during this eighteen-month absence.

By the time Irish affairs had settled sufficiently for people to sleep easily at night, the de Valeras had five sons and two daughters. Dev was the undisputed leader of Republican Ireland and Sinéad was able to revive her cultural interests. As a teacher, her special interest was always children. She wrote plays, poems and fairy stories in Irish and English and did fine translations from French and English. Sinéad de Valera died on 7 January 1975, the day before her sixty-fifth wedding anniversary. Dev died seven months later.

Aerial view of Dublin Port

12

Discovered –
but it was never lost!

Temple Bar

BEFORE the architects and the tourists, before the musicians and the artists, before the carefully cool business houses, it was there. It didn't need to be 'discovered' because it was never lost. Before it became our Left Bank, Temple Bar was a discreet, unsung part of town. This grid of old narrow streets drew certain kinds of Dubliner – the philatelist, the seeker after bargains in spectacles or timepieces, the quiet sportsman in search of a new rod or small rifle. They came to the little specialist shops which had been in their families for generations. And before that . . . Temple Bar has many befores.

In medieval times the land upon which the district now stands was hardly there at all. The Liffey's bank east of the walled city was a good deal further back to the south.

What land there was was held by the Augustinians, a south-side power even if Christ Church was the domain of Arroasian canons who occupied a doctrinal niche somewhere between them and the north-side Cistercians. As the development of Dublin marched eastward, the old church lands slowly gathered buildings and tracks and, of course, more land. Piles were driven to firm up the well-watered earth and the riverbank advanced northward.

John Speed's beautiful 1610 map of 'Dubline' seems to show every road, church and house in the city of about 9,000 souls. The quaintly graphic image reveals that the cartographer didn't find a lot around Temple Bar – just a large three-masted vessel at anchor about where the Alamo restaurant and Gallagher's Boxty House now do business and, on land, an old soldiers' hospital, a new bridewell and four or five houses on a track which would become Dame Street.

About twenty-five years later the street's early residents were joined by Sir Christopher Wandesford. He had a fine new house built for himself with a generous garden of apples, berries and flowerbeds sloping right down to the water's edge. About this time it was decided that Dublin was becoming substantial enough to need a Custom House. It was erected at considerable cost at the most logical spot of the day – on the seaward side of the city, on the south bank, of course, since Dublin was then largely a south-side place.

From 1621, the Custom House redefined these parts. The channel was always clogged with ships, often up to six or eight deep in the immediate vicinity of the new wharf and crane. With the extra ships came extra sailors and their raffish, dangerous lives. The houses followed and soon they were crowding in on each other in the narrow streets so characteristic of Temple Bar.

At Merchant's Arch was Bagnio's Slip, a perilous alley which led down to one of the river's first ferrymen. You took your life in your hands down there. Hard-drinking mariners fought dreadful brawls in these places along the quays – over women, over insults, over money, over nothing in particular.

Above: Ha'penny Bridge

These were the places where, thanks to the infamous press gangs, a man might fall into a drunken stupor to wake fighting the French in some distant war. These were the last places seen by chained men, women and children on their way to the Antipodes, some for nothing more than taking a trout from a river or an egg from a henhouse.

Temple Bar was, of course, much more than violence and disease. The immediacy of its contact with the outside world endowed it with a certain cosmopolitan atmosphere. Its taverns and coffee houses had an exotic air which drew a brisk business. The Custom House Coffee-House, run by John Cartwright and his wife, was honoured in street verse for its 'goods all both choice and sweet'.

An interesting early resident of the area in the mid-seventeenth century was William Petty, a medical doctor who had come to Ireland under Cromwell's banner. From a house in Crow Street he presided over an extensive survey of confiscated lands – and he helped decide what loyal supporters of Parliament would be rewarded. Not surprisingly, his house was soon known as the Crow's Nest. Years later, in 1683, Petty became the first president of the new Dublin Philosophical Society, which concerned itself with every rational subject from astronomy to animal husbandry.

The Crow's Nest became the base for these inquiring types and soon the house boasted a small botanical garden and a practical laboratory where inquiries were made into such diverse matters as telescopy, the nature of blood, poisons and various mutant cats, dogs and birds.

There was more fun about Temple Bar in the eighteenth century. The repressive puritan impulse had waned, making way for amusing profanities such as the theatre. Again Crow Street played its part. It was here that Dick Daly came in 1788. A likeable actor and general chancer from Galway, Daly had married wisely and soon found himself the owner of Smock Alley Theatre. In Temple Bar he opened his great hope, the Theatre Royal in Crow Street.

The venture went badly and in 1798 the city fathers, concerned at the state of municipal drama, persuaded Daly to hand everything over to their nominated man. Enter Buck Jones!

A man for the big impression, Frederick Edward Jones was convinced that he could become the darling of Dublin's cultivated class. Initially he spent about £1,000 refurbishing the theatre, but business was dreadful. These were difficult times: the French had gone mad with revolution and terror, Wolfe Tone was dead in Bodenstown, Robert Emmet had been hanged in Thomas Street. Jones thought people might enjoy the distraction of good theatre. He was wrong.

Life was too dangerous – and remained so. In 1819 he gave up and spent the rest of his time in Clonliffe House. They named the road after him. The Custom House had moved down river in 1791. Temple Bar lost its houses on the riverbank and got its quays. It also acquired the atmosphere that marked it until its current renaissance – a quiet district of respectable mercantile activity intermingled with houses of legal and financial men.

Down at the end of dog-legged Essex Street you can still see the charming exterior of the Dolphin Hotel, where gourmets once gathered to enjoy fine wines, famous steaks and majestic salmon in quiet mahogany peace. Dolphin House still carries the delightful stone details of its exterior, but inside are the joyless chambers of the Dublin Metropolitan District Court. Opposite Merchant's Arch, of course, there is Dublin's beloved Ha'penny Bridge where Bagnio's Slip once ran. This might have been the site of something much wilder – an art gallery spanning the Liffey similar to Florence's Ponte Vecchio. Designs for the gallery, which would house Sir Hugh Lane's collection, were prepared by Sir Edwin Lutyens in 1913 and there was decent support. This was as far as the suggestion went – after all, there were other things on official minds in that dangerous decade.

Lucien Bull

TRUE DUBS

HE was a sturdy nonagenarian when France paid an elaborate homage to him in 1966. Lucien Bull, a remarkable Dubliner, survived for six more years after his great day at the Conservatoire National des Arts et Métiers in Paris. He had marched with his adopted country at the forefront of some of the century's most exciting scientific advances.

Lucien Bull was born in 1876, the son of a supplier of religious goods in Suffolk Street. The still camera was the great gadget of the day and Lucien became interested. It wasn't long, however, before he moved on to his life's passion, the film camera. Having French family connections, the young man set off for Paris where wonderful things were happening in the field of cinematography. He managed to get a position as assistant to the great pioneer of recorded movement, Étienne-Jules Marey.

When the young Irishman arrived, Marey was already an old man with great successes behind him. In 1882 he had managed to record bird flight at the rate of twelve frames per second. By the time Bull arrived on the scene, Marey had achieved an incredible rate of 500 frames a second.

The young man carried on Marey's work after his death in 1904 with spectacular results. He became the great expert on ultra-rapid cinematography, shortly pushing the count up to nearly 1,000 frames per second. Through the years he made his cameras work ever faster until, by 1952 at the age of seventy-six, he recorded 1 million images in one second.

Lucien Bull went on to expand his range through optics, acoustics and several other related fields. During his life he held many of France's top posts in research, invention and cinematography.

13

Backwater full of surprises

(particularly for invaders)

Donabate

I T'S not dramatic like Howth. It's not spectacular like Dingle. It doesn't have a summit. It doesn't even have the almost-an-island quality which marks other peninsulas. We call it Donabate, although that is simply the name of the village at the centre of this little universe of winding roads, rolling fields, little woods and beautiful coasts. Although it's only 12 miles from the city, this charming district is surprisingly little known to Dubliners. This is really a peninsula of peninsulas. Shaped roughly like an arrowhead, it pushes out to sea trailing two offspring, north and south. All of which multiplies Donabate's capacity to produce places of utter peace. Talk about haunts of coot and heron!

You'll find yourself on a road that twists and winds with apparent purpose, only to be decanted at some beautiful backwater. You'll ramble over the fields aimlessly and suddenly find yourself looking down upon a Goldsmithian idyll of apple trees by ivy walls. Down by the sea you'll find a necklace of rocky coves where the ghost of Long John Silver would happily peg-leg about. The Donabate peninsula is a place of ancient frontiers. Hedges and long-forgotten tracks separate Donabate village from Turvey, Ballisk from Beaverstown, Rahillion from Portrane, Corballis from Kilcrea.

Donabate has always looked out in the direction of the raiders. The Romans, their tide so exhausted that Hadrian built a wall across England, may have briefly considered an adventure in these parts nearly 2,000 years ago. The evidence from the headland below Loughshinny a few miles to the north has yet to be fully assessed.

Less than a millennium later the Vikings came in off this sea to face the Irish. Neither race could show the other much that was new in the area of robbery, fire, torture and rape. However, the Irish probably held the moral ace – their cult of the anchorite, then at its apogee, was scattering its otherworldly message across a barbarous Western Europe.

One of the chief results of these encounters between Gael and Gall was the little, ever-beleaguered kingdom of Dublinshire which liked to include the arrowhead in its troubled sphere. It wasn't long before the Ostmen's Frankified cousins settled the question.

Before the end of the twelfth century Armoricus Tristram had bagged Howth and renamed his family after St Lawrence, on whose day he routed the Danish pirates of Sutton. Hugh de Lacy was lord of the cantreds of Meath and John de Courcy was ensconced in Ulster. The peninsula would be Norman, then English and deep within the Pale while that idea lasted.

The names of the old landholders told of their origins . . . in 1202 Geoffrey de Costentin from Normandy's peninsula, a little later the Barnewalls of a line which led back to the Breton 'Sieur de Barneville' who had been at the Conqueror's side at Hastings. The Barnewalls came and went in the story of Dublin and Ireland over the centuries. One Robert, in 1461, was made a baron by Edward IV and given the title Lord Trimblestown. His brother, Nicholas, became Ireland's chief law officer.

A century later Sir Christopher Barnewall seems to have arrived on the Donabate peninsula. After the Dissolution of Monasteries, the family had been granted the great convent of Gracedieu, the pride of female education in the Norman world which lay between Lusk and Swords. It is believed that Gracedieu was dismantled and the mansion at Turvey built from its stones. Again a century later another Barnewall was in the thick of political doings. Patrick was one of the 'Old English Catholics' who joined their Irish confrères in the 1641 rebellion against 'land-grapping'. For his troubles he was installed in the dungeon of Dublin Castle for stretching and twisting. The torture produced no admissions of guilt and so the Lord of Turvey was set free with the promise that his estate would not be plundered

Newbridge House, Donabate

by rampant soldiers. And again fifty years later Mathias Barnewall
fell foul of the Williamites at Limerick and found himself among the
Wild Geese fighting for France. Eventually, the Barnewalls toed the
religious line and remained at Turvey for many more generations.

On the way in from the main Dublin–Belfast road Newbridge
House demands a call. The old Cobb family seat passed into public
hands some years ago and is now in splendid shape once again, with
gardens teeming with interesting foliage and healthy wildlife. Another
of the peninsula's big houses, Portrane House, fared less cheerfully.
In the last century it was absorbed into one of those large Victorian
exercises in mental health.

St Ita's Lunatic Asylum was remote, out of sight, a virtual town
of gloomy redbrick wards and terraces where inmates endured what

passed for treatment in misguided times. Now a kinder place, which is more enlightened about the human mind, St Ita's still dominates the highest point on the peninsula.

Three miles to the east is the island which gave Portrane its name. Lambay was called *Reachrainn* before the Vikings came, so its little mainland pier was called *Port Reachrainn*. Time did the rest.

The place marks a coastal change of stroke. North is a lovely, long beach of grey sand, shells and solitude. South is a mini *côte sauvage* of caves and rocks and deep tidal gullies – with round tower and Martello nearby.

As the rocks peter out, there is the second Martello, standing as solid as the day it was built, at the end of the long straight down from Donabate village. The tower marks the start of one of Dublin's longest beaches, two silken miles ridged by rolling sand hills which sweep right down to the Narrows at Malahide.

And behind all this vigour of wind and sand and sea, behind the beaches that make the arrowhead are the two expanses of shallow tidal water which give Donabate its separateness and its peace. Haunt of coot and heron . . . and the occasional member of the human race.

Molesworth Phillips

TRUE DUBS

HE was a fresh-faced second lieutenant of marines when he embarked on the voyage of a lifetime. Molesworth Phillips was just twenty-one years old when he was picked to travel to the South Seas with Captain James Cook. It would be four years before he would return – without the most popular man in England of the day.

The great explorer had already made two long voyages of discovery which had given his country the overlordship of Australia and New Zealand as well as extensive claims in Antarctica and among the islands of the Pacific. When Cook's little convoy of sail left Plymouth on a sunny July morning in 1776, neither he nor his young companion from Swords, County Dublin, had any way of knowing that James Cook would not be coming home.

The expedition's quest was the North-west Passage, the elusive sea route from the Atlantic to the Pacific over the northern coast of Canada, which had claimed many lives before and after. However, it was not the ice or the freezing sea, which took Cook. The expedition pottered up along North America's western coast and pottered down again. The years came and went and in the winter of 1778 Cook decided to lie up at the Sandwich Islands, now Hawaii. Relations with the islanders became inflamed early in the new year when a small boat was reported missing. An encounter took place on a beach on St Valentine's Day, the islanders and the British facing each other belligerently. Fighting erupted and soon James Cook and all but two of his marines lay dead on the sand. One of the survivors was the young man from Swords who, though badly wounded, swam to safety.

Reports of the events preceded Molesworth Phillips to England and when he finally arrived back he was honoured with a captaincy and feted by London society. He lived to the age of seventy-seven years, acquiring along the way an estate at Ballycotton, County Cork, a home in London and the rank of brevet lieutenant colonel.

Cholera took him in Lambeth in 1832.

14

A stroll in the halls of history

Museums

I T'S not so much a hill, more a gentle rise that is over almost before it begins. Coming along Suffolk Street you hardly notice the incline, although Church Lane leading up from Dame Street is steep enough.

St Andrew's Church has been here or hereabouts in various forms for over 900 years, but it can seldom have looked better than it does today. The outer wall and railing have been removed, leaving a clean, open approach and allowing the building to put a little distance between itself and the commercial hurly-burly all around. The 1866 building has been given an affectionate once-over and is now a graceful pit stop for tourists wanting to know what's worth seeing. Dubliners who like the old town will also enjoy the new accessible St Andrew's, now so elegant and enlivened with the tintinnabulation of Italian, Spanish, French and German. Bells have been rung here since the beginnings of Dublin as a city . . . and necks.

Leinster House sits in the middle of a remarkable nest of museums

A grant of 1240 to one John Thurgot mentioned 'Thengmotha in parochia S. Andrea' in passing. This was the site of the Thingmote, the terraced parliament hill built by the Vikings soon after they arrived in the ninth century. Here they came, the king taking the highest seat, to make their decisions, to receive embassies from other Viking settlements and to break the bones of Irish prisoners taken in the endless wars of the times.

If you want to visit the Thingmote today, walk east from St Andrews and it's under your feet. The 40-foot-high mound was levelled in 1685 by a landed gent, Sir William Davis, who wished for more land. The soil was used to raise the level of St Patrick's Well Lane, the track which skirted Trinity College's south boundary. Within a decade the lane, now 8 feet higher and much more than a lane, would be renamed in honour of the Count of Nassau, more widely remembered as William III.

Up from Nassau Street there's another parliament hill where Leinster House sits in the middle of a remarkable nest of museums. In 1744, when James FitzGerald became the twentieth Earl of Kildare, this was a distinctly unfashionable part of Dublin. The streets and houses dribbled away across Coote Lane into swampy fields owned by the Viscounts Molesworth.

Leinster House, Kildare Street

FitzGerald knew his pulling power in the social firmament of the day. He'd make the place fashionable simply by living there. He hired Richard Cassels, the German architect who had already given Dublin several great buildings, including the mansion which would become Iveagh House and later he would design the Rotunda.

Cassels' brief was a house with a front at the front, a front at the back and the usual gardens. The project took two years and the result was splendid. It wasn't long before the carriages were queueing up to 'do a turn' of old Coote Lane, now grandly styled Kildare Street. About twenty years later FitzGerald became the first Duke of Leinster – and promptly renamed the house. Shortly after the Act of Union in 1800 the Royal Dublin Society (RDS) paid £10,000 for Leinster House and the collections began to gather. At first the house was sufficiently capacious to hold whatever the RDS felt fitted into its burgeoning notions of science and rectitude. The Society was especially fond of agricultural shows at which the latest ideas about animal husbandry and land use could be displayed. Henry Inglis, an English traveller, was greatly impressed with the 1834 show, although he was at pains to record his dismay at the sight of scores of ragged, barefooted children fighting over vegetables left half-eaten by the prize cattle.

By mid-century the country's ordinary folk were dying in their hundreds of thousands as the famines of the Forties tore the heart out of Ireland. At Leinster House, however, the large ambitions of the early Victorian age could not be accommodated. The gentlemen – and occasional gentlewoman – of science and philosophy were creating wonders still with us today. In 1853 William Dargan, the great Irish railway entrepreneur, staged the Dublin Exhibition under five glass domes on Leinster Lawn. Four years later the first of four museums, Natural History, made its appearance in a quiet granite palazzo erected by the RDS with state aid on the Lawn's west side. This delightful place is virtually unchanged, a monument to Victorian exuberance and taxidermy. The ground floor, where three Great Irish Elk skeletons lord it over fish and insect, is lit by the normal windows. Upstairs, where the creatures are more exotic, there are no windows. Instead, natural light streams in through the glass roof. Narrow

balconies lead you up above the mammals of Africa and Asia frozen in attitudes of solemn peace, up to the birds and the lizards and the extraordinary glass models of various obscure creatures.

Across the Lawn two years later the foundation stone of the National Gallery was laid, but it wasn't opened until 1864. At first the place was rather shy of masterpieces. Over the years, however, a succession of curators including George Mulvany and Hugh Lane built up the collection with purchases, grants and bequests – including George Bernard Shaw's gift of one-third of his royalties from *Pygmalion*, which extended posthumously to those from *My Fair Lady*.

Today the Gallery is deservedly top of the list for the cultivated student of art and art history. There are Rembrandts and Turners, Reynolds and Sisleys . . . and, of course, the famous Carravaggio of Christ's betrayal by Iscariot which hung unsung in a Dublin convent until it came to wider attention.

On the Kildare Street side it was thirty years before the companion Gothic set of the National Library and the National Museum were built. The RDS was still in residence – it remained there until the new state acquired Leinster House in 1924. The Society had passed its library to the country in 1877. It moved in 1890 to its new home with a sublime circular reading room.

At about the same time the treasures of the Royal Irish Academy were taken into official hands. In 1890 the chalices and the shrines, the gold ornaments of pre-Christian times, the skeletons of Ireland's

many yesterdays were installed in their new Palladian home of sandstone and marble. And the National Museum has been getting better ever since.

Dublin's museums are many and varied and ever-changing. They just won't fit on one page. Watch this space for further silent trekking on the north side, in the suburbs and elsewhere on the south side.

Catherine McAuley

TRUE DUBS

SHE was a child of eleven living in comparative comfort in County Dublin when France erupted in revolution. By 1798, the year of Ireland's dreadful turmoil, she was twenty years old and living with adoptive parents.

Catherine McAuley was a formidable woman, more formidable than the placid face on our £5 note would suggest. Her family life was Catholic and what might have been an unremarkable life changed dramatically when her parents died during her early teens.

In 1796 she was taken in by the Callahans of Coolock House, a wealthy Protestant family. The newcomer was to become much more than a daughter to the elderly couple. So impressed were they with her selflessness and integrity that they became Catholics too.

When William Callahan died in 1822, he left everything to Catherine who was then forty-four years old. She immediately bought a patch of land in Baggot Street and built a house for working women and a school for poor children.

Dublin at the time had lapsed into one of its periodic torpors, triggered by the Act of Union, which had closed the Irish Parliament and ended much of the intellectual life that went with it. Poverty was increasing as the population rose dramatically.

In the year of Catholic Emancipation, Catherine McAuley formally entered into religious life, at the Presentation Convent on George's Hill. She was fifty-three years old when she founded the Sisters of Mercy in 1831.

She lived ten more years during which her order grew and spread. It provided free education for generations of girls. It worked for the poor and especially cared for 'poor young ladies in danger'. The Sisters of Mercy eventually became one of the biggest religious orders in the world.

15

A nice place to be nowadays

Dublin Castle

IS there anything that hasn't been seen and felt inside the curtain wall of Dublin Castle in all its eight centuries? Pain, dread, fear, hatred, treachery – but also loyalty, love, affection and laughter. It depended upon who you were and when you were. In our time, there's been republican pride at European occasions and presidential occasions. And boredom at Beef Tribunal occasions, boredom such as could be relieved only by the cheering sound of lawyers' legs breaking.

The Castle has probably never looked better. The copper-topped Bedford Tower is now revealed as intended after the removal of a third storey added by an eighteenth-century philistine. The old Chapel Royal is in pristine Gothic Revival shape with the waxed devices of all the kings' men around the balconies. The courtyard pebbles, washed individually, sigh occasionally as a Mercedes or a Lexus rolls to a stop emitting a last puff of environmentally friendly exhaust. Between 1985 and 1989 over £20 million was spent getting the Castle into shape. If Ireland's 1990 European presidency was the spur, who's complaining?

Out of Dublin's Castle he rode, the Lord Deputy for England's Elizabeth, out through the portcullis to the hill that ran down from Christ Church, out on horseback with his soft hat, his baggy, striped knickers and thigh-high boots leading his helmeted cavalry. Sir Henry Sidney, in John Derricke's famous woodcut, setting off to do dreadful work for his Tudor mistress. It was the second half of the sixteenth century and English policy on Ireland had grown vicious. Elizabeth's father, Henry VIII, had executed Silken Thomas and his five uncles in the Tower of London in 1537 while the Geraldine women pined in the dungeons of Dublin Castle for their pampered lives in Maynooth and the vast Supremacy of Munster. The Tudors worried about Ireland.

They were small and jittery in a century belonging to Spain and Portugal. They envied and worried. Hadn't Ireland been conquered for England 300 years ago? Not quite. Right, they would complete the Norman half-conquest, sort out 'the English rebels' who had adopted 'barbarous Irish ways'. They would make Ireland's English and Irish dress like Englishmen, speak like Englishmen, think like Englishmen, obey like Englishmen. And they would break Rome's hold.

Sculpture outside the Chapel Royal, Dublin Castle

Henry made himself King of Ireland, issued the first Irish coins showing a harp and sent English Deputies to Dublin Castle to govern instead of using the usual local Normans. Elizabeth, throughout her forty-five years on the throne, continued to work through a line of merciless shipped-in Deputies. It was official frightfulness and Dublin Castle was always at the centre of events.

From his waxed oak desk in the tumbledown draughty Castle, Sidney wrote proudly in 1576 that he would not trouble the Privy Council with 'the name of each varlet' put down since his arrival 'but down they go in every corner and down they shall go'. Another Deputy, Sir Humphrey Gilbert, liked to 'bring great terror to the people' by making a lane to his tent with 'the heads of their fathers, brothers, children, kinsfolk and friends.' Edmund Spenser came to Dublin Castle in 1580 as secretary to the rampaging Lord Grey de Wilton, the Deputy to whom one didn't mention Glenmalure. The great poet spent seven years in and around the Castle, penning *The Faerie Queene*, making his reports and often campaigning with his master. The ethnic cleansing in Munster shocked him with 'anatomies of death . . . creeping out of every wood and glen on their hands for their legs would not bear them'. When the Elizabethan Lord Deputies were not off aslaying, they were complaining about the Castle which was described as 'ruinous, foul, filthy and greatly decayed'.

The dungeons 'for rebels and priests' were notorious, but hardly secure.

Many refurbishments were ordered, but the Deputies preferred to live elsewhere – in the Phoenix Park, in Kilmainham, in Lucan – leaving the epicentre of English rule to soldiers, record keepers, cartographers and torturers.

It was in 1204 that the construction of the Castle was ordered by King John. This son of Henry II had been styled Lord of Ireland at the age of ten in 1177. An unfortunate buffoon, he went down in history as John Lackland because he lost Normandy and was forced to sign the Magna Carta. In 1199 he appointed Meiler Fitzhenry as his Irish Justiciar, the same Meiler who had landed as a youth at Bannow Bay with the first Normans. Now a weary old soldier, he knew what was what when it came to defence. The site for the Castle had to be the confluence of the Liffey and the Poddle, where Irish, then Viking strongholds had stood in their day. Before the work was finished in 1215, the fragility of the little colony was demonstrated when the O'Tooles and the O'Byrnes struck from their secret Wicklow valleys.

The mountain septs, ever strong and hostile, rode down upon an Easter Monday fair in Cullenswood, where Ranelagh is today, leaving 500 Bristolmen dead.

From the beginning the Castle was a rambling, unsatisfactory affair. Its life buzzed around the royal offices, while the upper and lower yards were dotted with treasury, exchequer, armoury, arsenal, chapel and, of course, the essential apparatus of kitchen, buttery and mill. In 1234 a new ceremonial hall was added – its marble columns, dais, rose window, frescos of various monarchs and piped water made 'woeful Dublin Castle' the envy of Ireland.

The dungeons 'for rebels and priests' were notorious but hardly secure. Hugh O'Donnell, the great Red Hugh who made Gaelic Ireland's last stand alongside the even greater Hugh O'Neill, was locked up twice and escaped twice. The first time, in 1590, he was caught on the way to Wicklow. The second time, Christmas Day 1591, he made it to Glenmalure where Fiach MacHugh O'Byrne ruled without reference to Dublin Castle. O'Donnell made it home to Donegal, shy two toes taken by frostbite.

While the twentieth-century storm gathered over English Ireland, Dublin Castle had some of its biggest spenders. Lord Cadogan and after him Lord Dudley believed in ostentation, sparing no expense to make a success of 'the season' from late in January until St Patrick's Day. So they would come by carriage from privileged homes and mansions, the cream of society moving with haste through a city with the worst tenements in Europe.

Once in the arched gate of the Castle, it wouldn't be necessary to think about the world outside.

By 1921 the outside world had changed everything. In December of that year the last Lord Lieutenant, the Catholic Earl Fitzalan, saw two taxis arrive in the Great Courtyard. Michael Collins was taking possession of Dublin Castle for the new Ireland.

Frederick Maning

TRUE DUBS

THE *Pakeha Maori*! The Stranger Who Became Maori . . . what a title for a Dubliner! Frederick Maning didn't really see himself as a Dubliner. New Zealand was his country. He was there before it joined the British Empire and, after his death in London at the age of seventy-one, he was shipped back for burial. He began life in the western valleys of the Dublin mountains, in the modest farmhouse of Johnville above Saggart. When he was twelve, in 1824, his father decided that Van Diemen's Land was the place for his young family. So it was that young Fred Maning grew to splendid Antipodean manhood.

At twenty-one, he stood 6 foot 6 in his stockinged feet and weighed 16 stone. Van Diemen's Land wasn't big enough for him. He booked himself a passage on a schooner, which included New Zealand on its rounds.

Although it was seventy years since Captain Cook had claimed them for England, the islands had hardly been touched by the dread European hand. As Europeans went, however, Fred Maning was a very decent sort quite untouched by the age's mad missionary zeal. A man of famous good cheer, he was quite happy to adopt the life of the people about him. He got his own patch of land on the northern island, married a Maori woman, had several children and received tribal recognition.

The Dubliner was twenty-eight when London moved in 1840 to make New Zealand one of the pink parts in the world's atlases. He became a powerful protector of Maori rights as one of the first judges of the new order. He also wrote with affection and sympathy of his adopted people.

Whether the *Pakeha Maori* ever visited his native Dublin again is not known. It is known that he came to London as a sick, old man of sixty-nine. He hoped for a cure but his illness only worsened. In 1883 he made the return voyage to New Zealand in a coffin.

16

The mystery off our coastline

Lambay Island

IRISH island for sale ... Cecil Baring had picked up a copy of *The Field* in Munich. He was intrigued, as was his wife when he brought the paper home to their apartment. They contacted the agent and soon they were hurrying to Ireland by train and boat. The island, off the coast of north Dublin, would become their home.

It was in the spring of 1903 that the long peace of Lambay was broken by crews of masons, bricklayers, carpenters, painters and decorators brought in to make the old castle habitable. After that initial burst of activity, Baring, now Lord Revelstoke, hired Sir Edwin Lutyens, one of the great traditional architects of his day, to render the old fortress into a mansion with mock-medieval touches. The Barings were reportedly very happy on Lambay, welcoming experts who were interested in the island's history and wildlife.

Although no more than one square mile and only a half of that walkable, Lambay had no trouble holding the prisoners. Over 1,000 of them had been sent to Dublin's biggest island to find what shelter they could in the few rough huts or in the woods and fields that circled Knockbane. They were a small part of the defeated Jacobite army. Some had been at the Boyne the year before, but they had also tasted the sweetness of Limerick when the first siege was raised. Then at Aughrim, having nearly won, they lost the battle of the two foreign generals – their St Ruth from France and the Williamite Ginkel from the Low Countries.

Above all the generals and the kings, their favourite was Patrick Sarsfield, the courtly and courageous Dubliner now making the last stand for the Catholic side in Limerick. These men waiting out the last months of the war on Lambay had seen the great stylish form of their hero, all ermine and boots, fine hats and long hair, ride through their ranks preparing them for doomed battle. All had gone badly.

A Catholic restoration in England was now out of the question. James II was off whinging in France. Sarsfield would soon be there too. Their men summered on Lambay in 1691 awaiting the pleasure of the Williamites. The October peace was magnanimous enough, but the prisoners on Lambay were victims of a narrow-minded fraud. News didn't travel in the ether in those times, but by hoof, oar and sail. It was easy to keep the island ignorant of what had been settled at Limerick.

The treaty spoke of full and simple freedom to go in peace without penalty, but instead they were told they would be freed only if they swore allegiance to William. The prisoners did so and eventually left the birds and the cliffs for good. Whether they observed their oaths was irrelevant. Ireland was now officially Protestant and would remain so until the Church of Ireland was disestablished in 1871.

Islands make handy history, the smaller the handier, these stepping stones of history provided by nature as a toe-hold for the average invader. When learned John Tiptoft, the Earl of Worcester, was sent from England in 1467 it was to Lambay he came with his force of 700 archers. Learned he may have been, but he was also murderous. At Lambay he ordered a castle, some walls of which still stand, and assessed the task in hand. His instructions from Edward IV were to sort out the most powerful man in Ireland, the Geraldine Earl of Desmond who was too friendly by far with a greatly revived Gaelic Ireland. Tiptoft accused Desmond and the other great Geraldine, the Earl of Kildare, of treason. They came to meet their accuser at Drogheda and, to the great shock of Ireland and much of Europe, Desmond was summarily executed on 14 February 1468.

'This treacherous Saxon earl' had been known as 'the Butcher' long before he came to Ireland. He followed the Earl of Desmond within two years – beheaded before a howling mob in England when his Yorkist masters were briefly displaced by the Lancastrians.

There can be little doubt that Lambay was inhabited since the beginning. The Irish named it *Reachra*, a name which survives in *Port*

Reachainn, Portrane. Ptolemy called it *Limnus*. The Vikings called it *Lamb Ey*, the island of lambs. It is certain that the dangerous elegance of the longships broke Lambay's northern horizon in 795. The watchers on Lambay can't have known it, but a more famous island far to the north had that same year also had its first dreadful visitation by helmet, sword and spear, by men with no knowledge of the ancient idea of sanctuary. Soon the unfinished Book of Kells was being hurried from Iona across sea and land to a safer place in the little Irish kingdom of Brega. In Rome Leo III made Charlemagne an emperor, but at Lambay the Vikings came and went, raiding, resting, honouring Odin and Thor, and telling of what they found. Perhaps it was on Lambay with its teeming fulmars, shearwaters and gulls that the bird boys refined their expertise in 837, while their elders prepared the longships for the great Liffey adventure ahead. It was high summer of that year when a war fleet of 65 vessels – top speed 12 knots under full sail – arrived up the lovely river. Life on the estuary was changed forever.

An old tradition speaks of the part played by the bird boys in the Viking victory. These children, orphans, urchins, catamites, were the youngest members of the crews and the most agile. Their masters commenced their actions by sending the boys off to catch small nesting birds. They made weapons of the living birds by attaching lighting tapers to their legs and releasing them. The birds then carried fire back to the eaves of the little homes of wood, straw and reeds. It's an old tale which might or might not be true.

The population of Lambay was never large. It was probably near its peak at about 100 in the early nineteenth century. It had dropped into the seventies in 1854, when the island took the lives of four times that number.

The *John Tayleur* was a substantial vessel, a comfortable ironclad clipper especially built for the empire-building trade to Australia. It left Liverpool on 19 January with a crew of 120, mostly Chinese and Indian, and 450 passengers, mostly Irish. Blown off course, the *Tayleur* found itself facing Lambay's eastern cliffs two days later. It struck, broke free and struck again in violent winter storms. It was a day and a half before news reached Dublin. By that time, almost 300 people had been lost. Only about 100 bodies were recovered. They were buried behind church walls near the little harbour.

A few decades later the island became the private domain of the Barings, the German bankers of George III recently brought down by Nick Leeson's spectacular oriental betting binge. In 1911 Cecil Baring, Lord Revelstoke, shipped Sir Edwin Lutyens over to add some flourishes to the old island mansion. He also declared Lambay a sanctuary for wildlife. And there it is today. As for us ordinary Dubliners, we'll have to be satisfied with looking at Lambay Island from a distance.

Seán Lemass

TRUE DUBS

BY bike through the Phoenix Park he would go, the Minister for Supplies showing people how to supply themselves free of charge with transport and fresh air. The bike was big and black, the gabardine light brown and fully furled, the wide hat pulled low and the pipe parked ready for a match under the moustache. It was 1944 and Seán Lemass, always a year older than the year having been born in 1899, was in his prime.

Behind him were the wild and dangerous years of the Easter Rising and the Civil War. Ahead were the high 1960s when he captained Ireland's cruise into the sun. This son of a Capel Street draper had always been unstoppable.

At O'Connell School he was a winning student and at the GPO he was a willing rebel. The national hurricane didn't disrupt his education. Economics and history were his passions and he read his way through prison libraries at Ballykinlar, the Curragh and Mountjoy.

He was just thirty-two when Éamon de Valera appointed him Minister for Industry and Commerce in 1932. It became his office – unless Fianna Fáil were out of office – until he was elected Taoiseach in 1959.

Although he had gone through the fires for the principles of the new Republic, Seán Lemass was never bitter or dogmatic. His great mark was his pragmatism, his refusal to let old shibboleths stand in his way. He surprised – and delighted – the world in 1965 by going north to meet Sir Terence O'Neill. It was a brave step by these two men, a step that set off a train of events which is still rolling thirty years later.

Seán Lemass left public office, having resigned, two years after the historic meeting. He died in 1971.

Slowly getting back
to its former glory

O'Connell Street

IT has length, width, life and history . . . but does it have class?
O'Connell Street, the centre of this famous little republic of
ours, has seen better days. But, to be fair, it has also seen worse.
Back in the 1920s the new state vowed that Dublin would have a
street fit for a capital. Six years of revolution and civil war had left
the elegant half-mile in a sorry state, two thirds of its buildings in
ruins. The new government was slow to deliver and O'Connell Street
scrambled back to its feet thanks mainly to the city's masters of
commerce.

To be fair, the street's centrepiece, Francis Johnston's colossal
Graeco-Roman temple to Mercury, had been restored by 1924. That
was just eight short years after Patrick Pearse, James Connolly, Tom
Clarke and younger rebels, including a sixteen-year-old schoolboy
named Seán Lemass, had been taken from the gutted shell.

Miraculously, Miss Hibernia survived 1916. She stands there on top of the GPO to this day, massive beckoning breasts, spear newly gilded, stone skirts still as ever, flanked by Mercury and Fidelity. The trio have been there since 1818. For 148 of their years they eyed Horatio Nelson a few yards away. The admiral too was larger than life, standing a full 13 feet of Portland stone over the Pillar of 134 feet. The victor of Trafalgar had no particular connections with Ireland, but in 1805 Dublin was subdued and defeated. The Irish Parliament had been closed and the country brutally copper-fastened after the volcanic events of the previous decade.

In such times commerce is a people's therapy. So it was that Dublin's merchants, grateful to have the sea safe again for trade, passed the hat around. The Doric column ran to a reasonable £6,857 and a further £312 went on the statue by Cork sculptor Thomas Kirk.

The Nelson Pillar was, indisputably, the centre of Dublin, a place of rendezvous and assignation, the terminus for almost every tram in town. In 1966, presumably to mark the fiftieth anniversary of the Easter Rising, hard-hearted men removed the ancient mariner, it is rumoured with the aid of an explosive Breton. O'Connell Street has never been the same. No longer can Dubliners ascend the spiral stairs, panting and counting all the way up to sunlight and a dizzying panorama of the city.

For years after it had vanished, people still made arrangements to meet at the Pillar. Today all that's left are memories and Nelson's head in the Dublin Civic Museum. In the dark days of the 1960s and 1970s, when all the world was young, O'Connell Street was again betrayed. Its unrealised potential as a most noble thoroughfare was traded off in an orgy of tatty plastic and gaudy colours. Ice-cream parlours and fast-food joints engulfed the street.

Since the millennium year, however, the street has hauled itself back from awfulness. The Gresham and the GPO, pockets of grace from other days, have survived the worst and now look quite splendid in a streetscape that is improving all the time. If you're going the full length by foot, the best route is the island of trees, handsome lamp posts and decent statuary running all the way from O'Connell Bridge to the Rotunda. And, appropriately enough, it's Daniel O'Connell himself who mans the gates from his dark pile of winged angels, hounds of Banba, harps that once, swords of light and assorted peers, prelates and horny-handed sons of toil. The artist, John Henry Foley, didn't live to see his work in place. A Dubliner, Foley was regarded as the greatest sculptor in Ireland or England in the mid-nineteenth century. Clearly he was the man to do Ireland's great monument to the giant of the age who had shown what great changes could be made without resort to arms. Foley got the commission in 1866 but, sadly, had only reached the stage of full-size clay models when he died in 1874.

It was eight more years before the work was completed. As the century opened Dublin's main street had two names: the official one and the popular one. Your preference depended on your view of the national question – only to be expected in a city divided by so many lines drawn on the basis of religion, wealth, education, privilege and political beliefs. Luckily for Ireland, there were always people who crossed the lines.

When John Speed published his map of Dublin in 1610, there was nothing to record east of St Mary's Abbey. By 1685 Thomas Phillips could record Capel Street, Abbey Street and Great Britain Street. The north side was inching eastward, but it was the middle of the next century before Sackville Street appeared on the city's web. In 1750 Luke Gardiner inherited a street running from the spot where Parnell now stands to the place where Nelson once stood. It was named after Lionel Cranfield Sackville, the Lord Lieutenant. Banker Gardiner decided that it needed air. He demolished the west side and built a line of new houses 150 yards from the east side. Down the centre he laid out Gardiner's Mall where the street's new residents – MPs, lawyers, medical men, nothing but the best – could promenade with their families beneath the elms, by the obelisks and globes and other eye-gladdeners.

It was a great success and it helped to pull Dublin's centre of gravity to the east.

While Luke Gardiner was laying all this out, the wonderful, dreaded Wide Streets Commissioners were exercising their writ at Dublin Castle and Dame Street. Virtual dictators armed with frightening powers of compulsory purchase, they had often resorted to stripping the roofs from occupied houses which they wanted down. By 1785, when they took Sackville Street into their imaginative sights, nobody stood in their way. They decided to sweep right down through narrow Drogheda Street, through the old houses between Abbey Street and Bachelors Walk, through to the river where a new bridge was planned. As it turned out, Carlisle Bridge was finished in 1795, before Sackville Street reached it.

Along O'Connell Street there are signs of an ebbing of the tide of tat. It's slow but it's building. Shopfronts are getting better. The pedestrian island can be very pleasant on a sunny morning, running from the Liberator's elaborate memorial past William Smith O'Brien of the rebellion of the cabbage garden, Sir John Gray of the Vartry water, Father Theobald Mathew who fought the demon drink to Charles Stewart Parnell's more discreet furniture.

O'Connell Street still needs much work. And, unfortunately, the strange, gargantuan Anna Livia will never replace the admiral.

The Anna Livia monument was removed in 2001 to make way for the Spire of Dublin. It was relocated to Croppies Memorial park in 2011.

Christian Davies

TRUE DUBS

WAS it all in her imagination? Did she serve as a dragoon in the Royal Inniskilling Regiment? Was it possible that a woman could tramp around the Europe of Louis XIV in a soldier's uniform fighting at Blenheim and Nimwegen?

Little is certain about Christian Davies, except that she was born in Dublin in 1667 and died in poverty in London in 1739, at the age of seventy-two. Her life story appeared a year later. Although *The Life And Adventures Of Mrs Christian Davies* was billed as an autobiography, the identity of the author is open to doubt. This shouldn't be allowed to spoil a good story. The book tells a riveting tale of a young woman of obvious spirit.

Having inherited a tavern, Christian falls in love with a member of her waiting staff, one Richard Welsh. They marry, but bliss is denied our heroine. Welsh vanishes.

A year's silence is broken by news from Flanders . . . a letter to say that he had fallen foul of the press gang and been forced into the army. Christian, no faint-hearted thing, enlists, calling herself Christopher and embarks on a thirteen-year, continent-wide search for her beloved Richard. Fate finally smiles, giving them three years together before he expires on the field of Malplaquet. Queen Anne, tickled by her story, awards her a shilling a day for life.

At this distance, we'll never know the truth about Christian Davies. But it's a good story.

18

The Sands of Time

Sandymount

NOTHING around you for a kilometre in any direction. Nothing made by man, that is. Only the endless sands of the South Bull and the little waves of low tide fidgeting about as they start the six-hour trek back to the sea wall. You're in Dublin City. You're nearly 5 kilometres from O'Connell Street, but the solitude is almost perfect: just you, the waders, the gulls and the occasional dog unleashed by a distant master being driven wild by the funky aromas of the endless flats.

It's a rare district of Dublin that has such well-defined boundaries. With Sandymount, you know where you stand. To the east there's the sea, to the west the railway, to the north Irishtown. There's no south because it tapers away into Merrion where the railway meets the sea. Today Sandymount wears its village civility most naturally, but it wasn't always so. Before the railway came through on its way to Kingstown in 1834, it was rude and rustic.

A decent hotel and several hostels provided accommodation for those who came to this carbuncle on the coast noted for fine cockles, bracing air, golden sands and naked bathers. William Ashford, the landscape painter, arrived in the area in 1780. He had come to Dublin from Birmingham at the age of eighteen and rapidly established a lucrative reputation, earning enough to hire James Gandon to do him a sweet villa by the sea. It's still there as part of the Rehabilitation Institute.

Notwithstanding Mr Ashford's arrival in Sandymount, Dublin didn't see much reason to come this way and there were a few reasons to give it a wide berth. From medieval times the district was separated from the city by the lawlessness of Beggars' Bush where the dispossessed, the diseased and the dangerous lived off the pickings of innocent travellers. During the eighteenth and early nineteenth centuries, headquarters for the highwaymen and smugglers of Beggar's Bush was Lefevre's Folly, a ruined mansion engulfed in ivy and bushes on a slight eminence. From its ragged upper walls, watch was kept on several visible roads.

Nobody complained if their victim happened to be an excise man riding out to check George Haig's disreputable distillery on the corner of the Dodder where Marian College now stands. Mr Haig made good whiskey but the word around Ballsbridge and Sandymount was that quite a few unwelcome visitors had disappeared in his extensive property. All we know for certain is that when the railway arrived, the distillery went out of business.

Sandymount was cut off from the city by the highwaymen of Beggar's Bush

Before Mr Haig, before Mr Ashford, Sandymount was called Scald Hill if it was called anything. It was part of a network of old Bagod and Fitzwilliam fields which stretched right in to St Stephen's Green. Streams called the Nutley and the Trimlestown fed two sizeable lakes, one big enough to include within its compass the present sites of Sydney Parade Station and the lovely yellow-brown Church of St John the Evangelist. In 1750, before the Wide Streets Commissioners had begun their breathtaking work in the city, before Dublin had begun its dramatic expansion in every direction, Sandymount was little more than a tiny village huddled around 'Lord Merrion's Brickfields'.

A little distance away, where Seafort Avenue now reaches Beach Road, was the Conniving House, a thatched tavern famous for its fish dishes. In 1725 the proprietor, one Jack MacClean, got honourable mention in the reports of John Buncle, an English traveller who spent three days under his roof. The Conniving House was 'a delightful place of a summer's evening,' wrote Buncle, with 'matchless' fiddle-playing and bagpiping and 'the most agreeable of companions'. The inn was a regular haunt of Trinity students, who in those days could be very dangerous and quite beyond the law.

No doubt some of their more outrageous escapades were cooked up at the Conniving House over pitchers of ale and platters of cockles and mussels. Sandymount as we know it began to take shape when the railway permitted a second out-of-town home for those who could afford it. Rapidly from the middle of the last century the mansions marched south along the coast, followed by the suburbs. Soon the place where the brickmakers lived had become Sandymount Green, a kindly little triangle surrounded by humanely proportioned Victorian terraces. The churches followed. In 1850 the Herbert family dipped into their deep pockets to pay for the building of St John the Evangelist for the growing Church of Ireland congregation. Expense was not a point, so gorgeous biscuity stone was shipped in from Caen. It hasn't weathered well down the years: Sandymount's climate is clearly more moist and salty than that of inland Normandy. Happily, refurbishments are in hand and St John's front has been fully restored. Soon it will once again be the nicest church in Sandymount.

Three years later, in 1853, the great surge in Catholic church-building reached the area. The Church of Our Lady Star of the Sea took up position on the leafy corner of Sandymount Road. Eleven years later the Methodist church was built just off the Green, followed by the Presbyterian church in 1870; a century later the two congregations united. It was to Sandymount that James Joyce came after Oliver St John Gogarty evicted him from the Martello tower in Sandycove, to his aunt on Strand Road.

The year was 1904 and he was twenty-two years old. He'd had his fill of Ireland and had to get away. Soon he and Nora Barnacle were off in Zurich. From there ten years later, Joyce wrote to his aunt to know about the trees beside the Star of the Sea Church – he needed the information, and lots of other bits and pieces, for a book he was writing.

Poor James, she probably thought. He'd already been home twice. The picture house in Mary Street hadn't worked out at all. And then there were his stories about Dubliners – they still hadn't been published. Anyway, she and other members of the family sent him what he wanted to know, not dreaming that the little banalities would find immortality in one of the greatest books ever written in English.

John Dowland

TRUE DUBS

MUSIC stirred him, not politics. John Dowland was born in very political times in the little fortress town of Dalkey in 1562. It was an age of turmoil, a time of great and terrible things.

In Ireland, where the Tudor suppression was in full spate, the poet Edmund Spenser was telling of 'the anatomies of death' he had seen crawling on their hands and knees. In England Shakespeare was writing and Sir Francis Drake was hoping to emulate Ferdinand Magellan's voyage around the world. France was having its religious wars and in Italy Galileo had seen Jupiter's satellites in his telescope.

This was the Europe in which Dowland established himself as the greatest lutenist of his day. The plucked-stringed instrument shaped like half a pear had come to Europe by way of Moorish Spain.

In courts across Europe – from Paris to Leipzig, from Cologne to Antwerp – the Irishman established the lute as the great solo instrument of his day. Its popularity lasted about two centuries and it has been rediscovered in our time.

John Dowland's melodies and songs were immensely popular. He became a wealthy and famous man, mentioned by many contemporary writers. The King of Denmark hired him as court lutenist, paying him more than his chief admiral.

As profligate as he was successful, Dowland descended into gentile poverty. In old age he spoke bitterly of Ireland's lack of appreciation of his talents, of being unable to get any place at home. He died in London in 1626.

19

Our Botany Bay

Botanic Gardens

ONE fine day about 400 years ago, long before Europeans came to call the place Australia, a seed fell to earth in a forest on the other side of the world. By the time Captain Cook hove into view, it had become a fern tree of respectable age. It was well into old age when, thanks to the honourable tradition of botanical abduction, it found its way to Dublin. The gentlemen at Trinity College, who took it in, identified it as a passable example of *Todea barbara*.

About twenty-five years ago the fern, by now seriously geriatric, was moved again, this time to the Fern House at the National Botanic Gardens. And it's there to this day. It may not be one of nature's greatest works, it may look like something you'd whip out of the garden if you didn't know better, but, my, *Todea barbara* is venerable. The Botanic Gardens are only half as old. This year they celebrate their 200th year. The Irish Parliament had lots on its mind in 1795.

The Great Palm House, National Botanic Gardens

Relations with London were fractious, the French were behaving in their usual dangerous manner and rebellion was being preached in every second Irish alehouse and salon. However, Henry Grattan and his fellow MPs found time to direct the foundation of the Gardens on 27 acres which the Royal Dublin Society had acquired on the south bank of the Tolka River.

Five years later the parliament had voted itself out of existence, after much bullying, bribery and general badness. The Botanic Gardens fared better. Nature, even when made polite, has a way of seeing off people, parliaments, even nations. It now commands 47 lovely acres at Glasnevin, every one of them worth a visit.

First things first: the glasshouses! They draw you up the gentle hill from the entrance. There's no question of going any other way. They sit like spectral cathedrals, one dilapidated, the other pristine, both sublimely elegant. The men who made these things ruled the world in their day. Their Dublin was near the centre of a British world, of which they were intensely proud, a world which the Gardens have long outlived.

Glasnevin's first glasshouse was the Curvilinear Range, now fully restored and about to be filled with botanical immigrants. The project, done in stops and starts, ran from 1843 to 1869. It was the brainchild of Richard Turner, the great ironmaster of his day who invariably had several projects on hand at his Hammersmith works in Ballsbridge. 'Ubiquitous, always going about with daring projects in hand,' a friend wrote of him.

Queen Victoria saw the half-made project when she 'took a turn' of the Gardens during her 1849 visit. No doubt, Glasnevin made a welcome change from a down-at-heel city where the establishment had no apparent difficulty in turning its back on disease, dissatisfaction and dreadful poverty as famine engulfed the country.

The next project for the Botanic Gardens must be the saving of the Great Palm House. It desperately needs the sort of restoration which has just finished at its neighbour. The dilapidation is mainly evident, to the amateur eye, on the exterior – chipped paintwork, patched-up panes, warped woodwork.

Inside, however, it's still extraordinarily beautiful. Over the years since it was built in 1884, a spectacular collection of exotic trees and palms has been assembled, all kept at tropical temperatures which hit you like a blanket when you step inside. In all of Dublin there's hardly anything more calming, more soothing than to walk the quiet sweating paths under the vast foliage of this rain forest. If it's all fixed up, will the public be allowed up on the elevated walkways? That would be something!

The third in the Gardens' cluster of structures is the low hothouse which is home to the famous 400-year-old client from

Down Under, as well as every cactus you could imagine. But the prize in this neck of the woods has to be *Victoria amazonica*. It took nine years for Glasnevin to establish these giant lilies – an 1846 batch of seed failed to germinate and it wasn't until 1855 that the giant lilies began to propagate. They don't do much except astound, sitting on the still water, up to 6 feet wide with rims rising up 6 inches, capable of holding 200 lb weight if it's evenly distributed.

West and north of the glasshouses the acres open up handsomely. The walks wander through groves of cedar and oak, pine and maple and every other sort of tree. Roughly in the middle of everything is the Rock Garden – try and stop a kid running around its little paths.

Down by the Tolka you can start at the Rose Garden and work your way through the Mill Field and up to the high ground of chestnut, beech and alder. It's 200 years since Dublin acquired this place. And it's probably seldom looked better.

No finer place to plant yourself for a bright morning.

Exterior and Interior views of the Curvilinear Range

Brian O'Nolan

TRUE DUBS

ALTHOUGH a son of Strabane, County Tyrone, Brian O'Nolan must surely be counted an honorary Dubliner. A cultivated polymath, he placed the city firmly on the world map of droll literature. 'The kingly and melodious Irish' was, for O'Nolan, a perfect medium for the expression of original thought. He expressed his particular *Weltanshauung* sublimely in the ancient tongue – and as perceptively and wittily in 'base English'.

French, German and of course Latin were not unknown to him and readers of his emissions in *The Irish Times* were regularly tested as to the breadth of their erudition. In that paper he called himself Myles na gCopaleen. An example of his drollery: he received a letter from Lord Revelstoke taking issue with something he had written; in the manner of such folk, it was signed simply Revelstoke. Myles penned a fetching and bizarre response, which he signed simply gCopaleen!

After graduation in Celtic languages, O'Nolan obtained a position in the civil service. He worked in the Department of Local Government until, at the age of forty-one, he retired because of poor health. The drink was his demon: he couldn't function without it and, increasingly, he found it more difficult to function with it.

His great humorous fantasy was *At Swim-Two-Birds*. Having read it once, people turn again and again to this bizarre and wonderful melange of parodies on everything from student life in his Dublin to the bearded legends of old Ireland, from phoney Catholic piety to Irish pub life. This and other great opera made Brian O'Nolan an incomparable treasure for those who had discovered him.

For his books, he used the pen name Flann O'Brien. By whatever name you know him, he was an exquisite unique. Brian O'Nolan died in Dublin in 1966 – it would have amused him that he should have passed away on 1 April.

20

The Island that eventually joined Dublin

Howth

AFTER a hard medieval day of pillaging abbeys and hamlets, a Viking lay down to rest in the high heather. With a monosyllabic grunt he expressed his appreciation of the satisfactory massif on which he lay . . . and Howth was named.

No, it didn't quite happen that way. The Scandinavians were great men for headlands and their word for one was *Hoved*. Before they arrived, the old Irish knew the place as *Binn Éadair*, the Hill of Eadar, a battling chieftain of the De Danann.

War was never a stranger to the great peninsula reclining in indolent splendour at the top of Dublin Bay. Nor was love. Generations have come a-trysting and a-rummaging in its secret glades and tricky ravines, snapping twigs, disturbing rooks, dislodging stones. Most famously, there was that lusty pair of legend, Diarmuid and Grainne, who fled from the wrath of cuckold Finn to the moss of

Binn Éadair. Leaving myth aside, it is believed that 5,000 years ago, round about the time the magicians of light were building Newgrange, Howth was an island. A prehistoric rubbish pit found at Sutton indicates that the sea once flowed this way. Imagine the extraordinary tidal patterns that would have produced.

Ptolemy, working in the second century, made Howth an island with the name *Edri Deserta* in his map of these parts, but he was working on second-hand reports from sailors and traders. It's probable that by that time the isthmus had been well and truly established. The mark of man is light enough on the side of Howth facing Dublin. From a distance, gentle smudges of expensive housing break the foliage with occasional flourishes provided by the red and yellow Portmarnock brick of the Sutton Castle Hotel, the red limestone Martello and the white Baily Lighthouse. It's on the northern side that Howth declares itself. The old town languished for centuries in windy isolation, looking out from its tight little houses in narrow streets towards the island of many names – sometimes *Inis Faithleann* where Nessan built his hermit's cell, sometimes Eria's Island when the mysterious Eria made her home there. Then came the men from the north whose word for island was *Ey* – and so Eria's Ey became Erin's Ey and then Ireland's Eye.

Howth slept through the centuries until it was overtaken by the burgeoning mercantile pride of the early nineteenth century. A harbour was built and Howth was going places. The first stone was laid in 1807 and packets from England were soon coming in. In 1821 George IV came to view the new works – two impressions of his footprints were carved in a slab of the west pier.

Sadly, the Howth project was doomed. The powerful and capricious tides poured sand and mud into the haven and it proved difficult and costly to maintain enough depth for the ships from Holyhead. Dunleary won the day and Howth turned its back once again on the city. Soon the train came out from Dublin – and the tram, first by horse, then by electricity, beating its way along the coast road where highwaymen were almost as dangerous as winter waves. In our own time the Dart has made Howth newly accessible and the harbour has at last made a leap forward with its new yacht club, a pleasant and interesting modern building, and new eruptions of commercial activity along the East Pier.

The ambitious walker can do the circuit of Howth in a day, starting and finishing at Sutton Cross. No better time for the place than a bright, dry day in December with a few hefty sandwiches, a warming flask and an inch-to-the-mile map. Hugging the coast the houses grow grander, more individual, until the Cliff Walk leads down past the Martello to the series of southern inlets, Jameson's Cove, Shearwater and on to Drumleek Point.

Here the Baily comes into view beyond Doldrum Bay and the Lion's Head. Howth's first lighthouse was built on the summit during the reign of Charles II, but it spent most of its time illuminating mists. So in 1814 Dublin's port authorities, then happily rampant, nominated the logical place: the Duncriffan promontory where two millennia earlier a king called Criffan had built himself a fortress.

Break out the sandwiches here. North now, passing the steep, thickly birded eastern flank of Howth, a beautiful wild track which brings you past Gaskin's Leap, Fox Hole, Piper's Gut and Casana Rock. It was at Casana one freezing February night in 1853 that the steamer *Queen Victoria*, coming in from Liverpool with 100 passengers, lost its way in a blizzard. It was holed but managed to pull away, only to expire on the rocks below the Baily. Over fifty people were drowned. The episode didn't do a lot for Howth's reputation with mariners. Never mind: another sandwich and open the flask.

The home stretch from the Nose of Howth brings the northern panorama into view: Ireland's Eye, Lambay and the comely coast of the north county. The Cliff Walk threads west now past Balscadden Bay, where some still say the harbour should have been built, down past the Martello to the town and the castle. We're almost back where we began. It was in these parts that the old lords of Howth placed themselves on a saddle which commanded views in most directions except the sea to the east.

The first of the St Lawrences didn't bear that name at all. He was Sir Armoricus Tristram, who came from England for the

Normans' Irish adventure. He arrived at Howth in 1177, skelped the local Danish pirates on 10 August, the day of St Lawrence, and took the Spanish martyr's name for his family. A huge two-handed sword still kept at the castle is said to have belonged to Tristram. The castle is a pleasing hotchpotch of styles ranging over five centuries, from a medieval gate tower to an ersatz keep designed by Sir Edwin Lutyens.

The grounds have their treasures too. Aideen's Grave, an ancient dolmen where legend places the remains of a grief-slain beauty, once stood open to the sky but it's now engulfed by the rhododendron gardens which smother Carrickmore in pink, red, white and all kinds of purple at the right time of year. Howth isn't just for looking at from a distance.

Dermot McMurrough

TRUE DUBS

THE man who invited the invaders to come to Ireland – as schoolchildren we gasped at the treachery of Dermot McMurrough, forgetting that each and every one of us is descended from an invader of one sort or another. Dermot, King of Leinster, was a Dub but not one of whom the city was ever proud.

Born in 1110, he was a substantial man. He kept a house of stone in the city at a time when most folk lived in homes made of mud and twigs. He was also, obviously, an impulsive man of action. It was his liaison with Dervogilla, wife of a lord of Breffni, that was to change the course of Irish history.

Dermot abducted the good lady, although some suggest that she went willingly enough. Banished from his kingdom for his behaviour,

Dermot turned for help to Henry II, the Angevin king of England and half of France. Get me Leinster back, he said, more or less, and I'll forever be in your pocket.

Henry, never one to turn down a sure thing, agreed. A whole new island was thus opened to Norman gaze after their success in gaining control of England. In the way of canny kings, Henry didn't come himself at first. It was Richard de Clare who led the Norman excursion which was to transform Ireland.

De Clare, soon known as Strongbow because of his prowess with arms, landed in 1170, more than a year after his advance party. It wasn't long before he had taken Waterford – and Aoife, Dermot's daughter who had been promised by her scheming father.

McMurrough, it seems from the record, was a fairly ruthless sort for whom little was sacred. With Norman aid, he captured Dublin. A year later, in 1171, he died in Ferns 'without will, without penance, without unction' to be forever excoriated in the classrooms of Ireland.

Down by Anna Livia

Chapelizod, Lucan and Leixlip

JAMES DUFFY, who toyed heartlessly with Emily Sinico, was a cold and precise man. He didn't wish to live in the city, so he made his home in a sombre house in Chapelizod. Shem, Shaun and Isobel lived out here too with mother Anna Livia and their publican father, Humphrey Chimpden Earwicker. The proprietor of these fictional folk knew Chapelizod well . . . and Lucan and Leixlip. James Joyce, like so many Dubliners at the turn of the century, was on intimate terms with the city's gentle, riverain approach.

Sheridan Le Fanu, the great nineteenth-century journalist and master of the macabre, gave Chapelizod its finest fabricated flourish. *The House by the Churchyard*, his long tale of dreadful doings, is set in a Chapelizod bathed in rosy, rustic nostalgia. It never did take much to persuade day trippers to these parts. If the sun shone at all on a Saturday or a Sunday during the nineteenth century, apparently, people headed west in large numbers, some by carriage, some by foot, through the Phoenix Park and out along the little roads on the Liffey's northern bank. Being on the northern bank, it faced south and, in popular imagination at least, had a warmer climate than the rest of Dublin. How else would these favoured slopes between Knockmaroon and Lucan produce the Strawberry Beds? For a penny a portion, a young man and his sweetheart could take their places at one of the tables placed out by the families of the thatched cottages and treat themselves to strawberries and cream served on a leaf of cabbage. The strawberries are no longer there and the little tables no longer appear in fine weather. But three decent pubs – the Wren's Nest, Strawberry Hall and the Angler's Rest – hint of those lost times.

An Slí Mór, the ancient route from Galway, may have come into Dublin by way of the Liffey's southern bank, but the northern bank was nevertheless one of history's flight paths. Every manner of warlord – Irish, Norman, Tudor, Cromwellian, Jacobite, Williamite – came this way looking for trouble. Tristan was only a messenger boy when he came, but he found trouble. Sent by King Mark of Cornwall to seek the hand of an Irish princess, he found more than a hand – which didn't please Mark. Iseult's father, King Aenghus, built a chapel for his tragic daughter and down the years since then the name has melted from Chapel Isoulde to Chapel Ysonde to Chapellizard, and eventually Chapelizod.

Did it ever happen? Maybe not, but historians accept that Aenghus, Iseult and Tristan did exist. And the walls of St Laurence's, the Church of Ireland parish church, contain part of a sixth-century chapel.

There's no doubt that William III came this way. In the warm summer weeks after his success at the Boyne in 1690, he rested his Dutch bones at Chapelizod's viceregal lodge, a mansion with fifteen chimneys set in 200 acres by the river. Afterwards they called it the King's House – until the Artillery Regiment accidentally burned it down in 1832.

Two miles upriver was the home of William's most effective Jacobite enemy: Patrick Sarsfield grew to manhood in Lucan where this old English Catholic family had lived for centuries. They had undergone the famous process of Hibernicisation and, consequently, Patrick took his education at a military school in Angers, the old Angevin capital on the Loire. Sarsfield played his part famously in the war against the Williamites and, on bitter defeat, went with about 12,000 of his fellow Wild Geese to fight for France in 1691. He died far from Lucan, after a minor battle at Landen in Flanders two years later. Sarsfield's niece, Charlotte, inherited the estate and it passed on to her husband, the splendidly named Agmondisham Vesey. The old castle fell into ruin and the Veseys built the Palladian mansion which is now the home of the Italian ambassador.

A great priest in a famous fury rode out this way from Dublin in 1723 – a long enough journey for a man of fifty-six years – from St Patrick's Cathedral out past the dunghills by Usher's Island, across Bloody Bridge and then west past the gravel pits opposite the great hospital which Grizell Steevens was building.

Jonathan Swift was on his way to Marlay Abbey in Celbridge and he was angry. Esther van Homrigh, whom he called Vanessa, was half his age but she had followed the celebrated Dean from London and was determined to be the woman in his life. She drew him to her mansion set in silky riverside acres, to her bower by the waters. This day, however, Swift had no dalliance in mind. The other woman in his life, Esther Johnson, whom he called Stella and who may have been his wife, had just shown him a letter she had received from the mistress of the Abbey demanding to know the precise nature of her relationship with the Dean. So it was that the ageing cleric bounced out to Celbridge, tossed the letter down in front of Vanessa and strode out, never to see her again. The poor woman died, it's said, a few short weeks later of consumption. Her home became known as Celbridge Abbey and is now in the compassionate hands of the Brothers of St John of God.

On the other side of Celbridge is Castletown House, the biggest house in Ireland. This colossal pile, the most extraordinary place in all the Liffey valley, was erected by wealthy William

Castletown House, Celbridge (OPW Castletown)

Conolly, Speaker of the Irish Parliament, in the early eighteenth century. Its sheer size can be best conveyed by the telling windows ... almost 300 at last count. Sitting among the limes, the beeches and the oaky oaks that dawdle down to the river, it is a vast grey liner becalmed on a green ocean. Inside are staircases to take your breath away, gorgeous chandeliers from Venice, moody echoing corridors and fabulous statuary and plasterwork. Watching over the treasure is the Castletown Foundation.

History lies piled up on the riverrun into Dublin. Everywhere you turn you're following in the footsteps of warriors and lovers, thinkers and doers. They have all been charmed by these sweet tracks by the Liffey. Yes, the place has mileage.

Sheridan Le Fanu

TRUE DUBS

DUBLIN was rebuilding its intellectual life after the Union's damage when Joseph Sheridan Le Fanu was born in 45 Dominick Street in 1814's late summer. Reverend Le Fanu educated his son himself and then identified the law as an appropriate profession. At Trinity College, young Le Fanu's creative powers soon showed themselves. He wrote ballads and pieces in the *Dublin University Magazine*, which had just been founded by Isaac Butt, another priest's son studying law at the time.

Le Fanu was twenty-five when he stopped pretending to be a lawyer and embraced journalism. He threw himself into the creation of a strong evening paper for the city: the *Evening Mail*, a merging of three older titles, was a great success and was perceived as Dublin's own paper right into the early 1950s.

Le Fanu was sociable, witty, cultivated and cheerful, but there was a darker talent which became increasingly evident. In 1838, when he was twenty-four, he had made his first contribution to Gothic literature, *The Ghost and the Bone-Setter*. However, it was twenty years before the macabre took over his life.

His wife died when he was forty-four. A fitful sleeper and extensive dreamer, she often regaled him with her nightmares – no doubt some turned up on his pages. Her passing seems to have driven him from society. He retired behind the doors of 70 Merrion Square and there indulged his tastes for green tea and ghostly stories.

Within five years his novels began to appear. Chief among them, by general agreement, was *The House by the Churchyard*, recently reissued by Appletree. A monumental work full of character, incident and observation, it tosses extortion, murder and occult doings into the bucolic paradise of Chapelizod in the late eighteenth century.

Carmilla, his elegant story of vampirism, was not as popular. However, around about the time that Le Fanu died at his home in 1873, a young Trinity graduate in his twenties was reading it. Abraham Stoker would displace Le Fanu as the undisputed Irish master of the macabre.

22

The Best Mile in Dublin

St Stephen's Green

ONE side of the Irish political world in the first decade of the century called it the Fusiliers' Arch. The other side called it Traitors' Gate. Almost a century has passed and now Dubliners seldom call it anything, apart from 'the arch on the Green', if pushed.

As triumphal arches go, the Boer War testimonial is small but perfectly formed. It marks the start and the finish of one of the best even miles in Dublin. The arch was erected on the corner of St Stephen's Green in 1907 to honour Dublin men who died for England while the Irish Revolution was brewing. About 200 Fusiliers, most of them from the city, died in battles and skirmishes at places with long-forgotten names, places like Tugela Heights, Colenso, Ladysmith and Hartshill.

Fusilier Francis Dunne is not listed on the arch, because he came home to Dublin for a long life. 'The Bugler Dunne' was a child of fifteen years who followed his father into the city's famous regiment.

One warm South African December day in 1899 at Tugela he filled his lungs and blared out 'Advance' when he realised that his fellow Fusiliers were responding to 'Retreat' being sounded by a clever Boer bugler. Dunne's spontaneous action entered the imperial storybooks, as did his explanation: 'The Dublin Fusiliers never retreat.' Like much else of that Irish world, the Fusiliers were on the wrong side of history. Nine years after the arch was unveiled, bullets flew about this corner of the Green. Michael Mallin, once a drummer boy in the British army, commanded the College of Surgeons for the revolutionaries with the help of Constance Gore-Booth, the Countess Markievicz, in her proud green uniform.

It's difficult to imagine the days when St Stephen's Green was the fag end of Dublin, when a citizen put his or her life in great peril to go near the place. Until a Guinness decided that the city could do with a decent park, the Green was anything but green. The place was rather less than polite when Lord Ardilaun, otherwise Arthur Edward Guinness, dipped into his deep brewer's pocket, had a small heaven laid out on these 22 acres and presented it all to the city in 1880. In medieval times the hospital of St Stephen cared for lepers and other outcasts – but at a safe distance on these open lands well to the east of the walls. It was

1635 when the city fathers decided that Dublin needed open spaces: in front of the new Trinity College, at Oxmantown and at the Green.

William Petty, blessed with the gift of numbers, came to Ireland with Oliver Cromwell to measure and count and distribute. His 1655 map noted the Green's existence at more than twice today's size. In 1664 the city staked out 27 acres and within five years the Green had been levelled, ploughed, planted, walled and ditched. A century later the Green had begun to accumulate its surrounding houses. The German architect Richard Cassels had designed No. 80, which is now absorbed into the expanded Iveagh House. On the far side mean Coote Lane had become Kildare Street after Cassels built the fine house of the Earl of Kildare, whom society soon followed to this part of town. Belles and young bucks may have disported themselves on Beaux Walk, the Green's north side, but the park itself was still no Eden. The city allowed the Green to be used for concerts and various festive occasions, which of course attracted the attention of opportunists and undesireables.

In 1762 a scribe recorded some of the contents of the surrounding ditch: 'Dead dogs and cats bloated and drenched in mud.' In 1806 it was noted with sadness that the Green had lost many of its trees after a particularly dangerous fireworks display. This was the Green of the Emmets who lived on French Walk, the west side. Robert Emmet was the Viceroy's doctor and, as 'a man of condition' would not have allowed his sons, Temple, Thomas Addis and Robert, to use the Green except under close supervision.

Young Robert was taken by much greater dangers in Thomas Street in 1803 at the age of twenty-five. At the same time Charles Maturin, clergyman and Gothic novelist, was living in York Street around the corner from the new College of Surgeons. Friends often braved the weed-choked gravel tracks of the Green to reach his bizarre afternoon dancing parties which eventually left him bankrupt.

Things hadn't improved much when William Makepeace Thackeray passed this way thirty years later. He found 'lazy carmen . . . moaning beggars . . . and a fellow with a toy and book stall'. No doubt today's Green would delight a visitor who knew it in the past.

Admittedly, we've lost some treasured buildings, but enough have been saved and the park is certainly more civilised than at any time in the past.

It was on the south side, old Leeson Walk, that the ill-fated experiment of a Catholic university was tried. No. 86 had been built in 1765 for Richard Chapel Whaley, a Protestant bigot whose middle name soon became 'Burnchapel'. His son, Thomas, is more fondly remembered as Buck Whaley who walked to Jerusalem and back to win a wager of £40,000. The house was acquired in 1854 and John Henry Newman, an English convert to Rome, was placed in charge of the ambitious project. It foundered on various rocks, including its inability to award recognised degrees and disagreement over lay involvement. It was twenty years before an effective alternative to Trinity College was provided. For Newman they were years of tension and disappointment, but they also gave Dublin the charming Byzantine gem of University Church. The college-maker had brought Hungerford Pollen, another new Catholic, over from England to be his professor of fine arts. Pollen was invited to do a college church and given his head. He clearly took it.

Heading up towards Harcourt Street we pass the handsome pillars of the Smurfit Paribas bank, which once announced the Methodist Centenary Church. Until 1969 Wesley College was behind it.

The charming tucked-in Unitarian Church of 1860 sits lonely, dwarfed but undefeated among the new buildings that start the Green's east side. Just beyond in his own mini-Green is Lord Ardilaun, the Guinness who decided to clean up the Green and hand it over to the public.

The north side, where the beaus paraded under the lime trees, is always the liveliest. First there are the clubs where money and what passes for class mingle, cruise and dine in noble rooms of deep leather, Cuban mahogany and high stuccoed ceilings. Even when nobody is smoking, there is a gentlemanly aroma of pipe-smoke. The atmosphere is echoed at the other end of old Beaux Walk. The Shelbourne Hotel with its comely Nubian guard takes its name from the Earl of Shelburne who built the first house on the site. The title derived from a patch of Wexford and the holder was son of William Petty, the Cromwellian inchworm.

No better place to wind up your exploration of St Stephen's Green. Afternoon tea, of course – or something stronger.

Tom Kettle

TRUE DUBS

Died not for flag, nor King, nor Emperor

But for a dream, born in a herdsman's hut

And for the secret scripture of the poor . . .

The moving lines, written by Tom Kettle to his daughter, are on his memorial in St Stephen's Green. Kettle was a decent nationalist who convinced himself that England believed in the freedom of small nations. He was right if Belgium was the issue but not Ireland.

Born in 1880 into a prominent north county Land League family, Kettle went to the Christian Brothers in North Richmond Street. Then it was on to Clongowes and the Catholic University. The law was his chosen field. He practised for several years before joining University College Dublin as its first professor of national economics.

The nationalist ferment of the day attracted him and he joined the Volunteers. The outbreak of European war in 1914 led him to postpone his hopes for Ireland. He took a commission in the Dublin Fusiliers and set about recruiting men for 'the war to save small nations'.

While Kettle went about what he saw as noble work, others were proceeding with Ireland's cause. He was not a party to the Easter Rising of 1916, which he regarded as the ruination of the dream of a free Ireland.

Embittered and disappointed, he demanded to be sent to the trenches where Europe's young manhood was slaughtering itself. Five months after the Rising, Tom Kettle died at the age of thirty-six leading an attack on Givenchy during the Battle of the Somme.

Hugh Lambert was born in Dublin on 27 May 1944, the eldest son of Hubert Lambert and Kathleen Farrelly and one of seven siblings: Carol, Brendan, John, Liam, Kathleen and Laura. He was married to Angela Byrne for thirty-six years. Their children are Alan, Paul, John and Sam.

He began his career with the *Evening Press* and *Sunday Press* in 1962 as subeditor. From 1971 to 1980, he was a film critic for the *Sunday Press*, when he became production editor of the paper. He was appointed editor of *The Irish Press* in 1987. The paper ceased publication on 25 May 1995. Until his death in 2005, after a short illness, he worked with *The Irish Times* in charge of production on special reports.

Discover Dublin consists of a series of pieces written for the south Dublin newspaper *The Leader* from November 1995 to March 1996.

Our deepest gratitude to Queenie Byrne, Chief Archivist.

Photography

John Lambert – Pages 10, 32, 35, 47, 50, 55, 58, 63, 66, 71, 87, 89, 102, 109, 112, 116, 120, 125, 130, 137, 140, 148, 164, 169, 172, 177, 180, 188 + 193.
Angela Lambert – Pages 24, 40, 43, 45, 74, 77, 78, 156 + 161.
Paul Lambert – Pages 92 + 94.

Photos licensed from shutterstock.com

Page 1 and cover (spine) – Laurent Adgie
Page 2 – Smolina Marianna
Page 9 – Morzolino
Page 16 – Sample Stars
Page 21 – Fireglopage
Page 28 – Dermot McBrierty

Page 82 – Ronald Semmick
Page 100 – David Soanes
Page 126 – Albert H. Teich
Page 185 – foto909
Page 191 – imagedb.com

RISING

A pencil of granite, a bird of prey
Noble focus of the day

Engines of wealth of yesterday
Bequeathed us this stately way

In stone forever, Dublin's ray
Of solid municipality

Reds and browns and manmade grey
The city, the past, the perfect day

Time washed down the years
This place crept into being
A thousand small victories for genius,
Greed, madness, veniality and luck

The perfect imperfections
Of all the piled-up years
For our astonished eyes

Hugh Lambert